God's Embrace

God's Embrace

Praying with Luke

TERRY HINKS

DARTON·LONGMAN+TODD

First published in 2012 by
Darton, Longman and Todd Ltd
1 Spencer Court
140 – 142 Wandsworth High Street
London SW18 4JJ

ISBN 978-0-232-52948-7

Phototypeset by Kerrypress Ltd, Luton, Bedfordshire
Printed and bound by ScandBook AB, Sweden

Contents

Introduction to Luke's Gospel

Look and pray

In June 2004 a precious icon was returned to Russia from safe keeping in the United States of America. Huge crowds came to welcome the icon of Our Lady of Tikhvin, as it was first brought to Moscow and then St Petersburg. *Pravda* reported the event in full, speaking of the huge numbers involved in the processions. Above all the icon was a focus of prayer. Orthodox tradition holds that the icon was painted by Luke himself in the first century. In fact, though this is historically questionable, the idea of Luke as icon painter is a powerful one. As Michel Quenot comments in his study on icons, 'Considered rightly or wrongly as the first iconographer, he (Luke) unquestionably wrote the very first "verbal" icon of her (Mary) depicting for us a sort of interior portrait.'[1] Icons are never simply paintings as in Western art; they are as much works of prayer and the Spirit as of human hands and have a key role within Orthodox worship. As Thomas Merton wrote, 'It is the task of the iconographer to open our eyes to the actual presence of the Kingdom in the world.'[2] They give us 'a glimpse of heaven'.[3]

Luke's gospel is a glorious icon (or series of icons) – a window into the heart of God, an invitation to worship, to pray and know God's presence. Too often we have seen it as a collection of words, ideas and beliefs to be understood rather than a picture to be prayed with. Luke is inviting us to experience the gracious embrace of God, through the reality of Jesus, the wise one, the gracious teacher, the forgiving Saviour, the risen Lord, the glorified one who shares the Spirit to lift up our lives in joy and loving service.

Luke invites us to look at the icon he has written in his gospel – the portrayal of Jesus, the author of life – and of Jesus' continuing work, through his disciples, followers of the way, in his second book, the Acts of the Apostles. He wants his reader – Theophilus, friend of God – to truly know what Jesus did and taught in his earthly ministry (Acts 1:4) and continues to do and teach through his disciples (Acts 1:1).

In gathering materials for his 'orderly narrative' it is thought by many scholars that Luke used the earlier Mark's gospel, some material that was also used by Matthew and other sources and traditions uniquely his own, as the basis for his presentation of the gospel. He worked carefully with these materials, respectful of their testimony, yet willing at times to adapt and rearrange materials to present his vision of the new dawn brought about by the life of Jesus. His own circumstances and those of his hearers no doubt influenced what he included, what he omitted and the way he edited his material. Convinced of the necessity and power of prayer, Luke gives special emphasis to praise and prayer within his gospel and continues this theme in Acts.

By looking attentively at what Luke presents to us, we enter into the dynamic of prayer and action that flows through the story. He invites us to watch Jesus as he prays, to listen to his stories, to identify with the pleas and prayers of characters within the narrative and to ask for that same gift of God – the Holy Spirit – that filled Jesus and was poured into his followers after his ascension.

Oscar Cullman describes Luke as 'the evangelist of prayer'.[4] Joseph Fitzmyer points out that Luke 'depicts Jesus at prayer more often than any other evangelist'.[5] Jesus is at prayer at each of the major turning points of Luke's story – at his baptism (3:21), at the choosing of the twelve (6:12), before Peter's confession (9:18), at the transfiguration (9:28), before he teaches his disciples to pray 'Father' (11:2), at the Last Supper (22:17), at Gethsemane (22:41), on the cross (23:34), at the moment he is first recognised as risen and alive (24:30) and at his ascension (24:50). Jesus regularly withdraws to remote areas to pray (5:16), spends the night in prayer in the hill country (6:12) and regularly goes out to the Mount of Olives when in Jerusalem (22:39).

It is on one such occasion, when Jesus 'was praying in a certain place', that one of the disciples asks him, 'Lord teach us to pray' (11:1) and Jesus responds by teaching them to say a version of what we now call the Lord's Prayer. For Luke, Jesus is the great teacher of prayer, instructing his disciples by word and example. As well as the teaching included in Mark and Matthew's gospels, there are parables about prayer unique to Luke, in particular the friend asking for loaves (11:5–8), the widow asking for justice (18:1–8) and the Pharisee and the tax collector (18:9–14).

The gospel opens with the answered prayer of Zechariah and Elizabeth and moves on to the great psalmic prayers in the canticles of Mary, Zechariah and Simeon, set in the context of the prayer life of the temple. It ends with the disciples 'continually in the temple blessing God' (24:52). Luke's second book then begins with the disciples in the upper room praying together (Acts 1:14). The inclusion of Mary among the group gathered there is significant, echoing her role at the beginning of the gospel. The early Christian community follow Jesus' example in seeing prayer as a priority and gathering frequently to pray together.

This vivid picture of people praying, of Jesus' challenge to all to be awake and alert to God in their lives, can inspire us in very different times to seek the same gift of the Spirit to pray with and in us. W. H. Auden wrote: 'To pray is to pay attention to something or someone other than our self. Whenever a man so concentrates his attention ... that he completely forgets his own ego or desires, he is praying.'[6] In a world that seems to be suffering from attention disorder we are being called to watch and pray.

∞

God of word and silence,
I will give you my attention.
I will pay the cost of looking beyond myself.
I will learn to pray.

In a world of attention disorder
I will look to see your presence.
In a world full of competing voices

I will listen for your silence and your word.
In a world hardened to reality
I will reach out to touch your truth.
In a world haunted by the stench of death
I will breath in your Spirit of life.
In a world of gluttony and hunger
I will taste your living bread
and gather your crumbs.
I will learn to pray.

∞

Praying to the Father of Jesus

'Christian prayer does not simply suppose "contact with the
divinity" or the absolute, but rather with the Father of Jesus, the
God to whom Christian faith and prayer is directed.'[7] Christian
praying has this very particular basis – in the praying of Jesus and
the relationship of trust and love Jesus summed up in the word
'Father'. Mark's gospel reports Jesus using the Aramaic word
'Abba' as he prays in the Garden of Gethsemane (and the apostle
Paul retains memory of this in Romans 8:15). Luke omits this
Aramaic reference in the same way as he omits the Aramaic 'talitha
cum' in the story of the raising of Jairus' daughter. But behind
each use of 'Father' in his gospel is that 'Abba' praying of Jesus.
This, as I explored in the first book in the series, 'is not patriarchal
language but relational language'.[8] Above all it draws from the
Jewish belief in the sacred covenant – that mutually committed
relationship of God to God's people and God's people to God.
Jesus summarises, personalises and renews that relationship in
addressing the mystery of God as 'Abba'.

Luke clearly saw the relationship summed up in Jesus' use of the
word 'Father' as more important than the word itself. In fact when
we look at prayer in his second book those prayers that are voiced
are directed to 'the Lord' and often, it seems, to Jesus himself. For
example, at the choice of an apostle to take the place of Judas (Acts
1:24–25) Peter prays, 'Lord, you know everyone's heart …', and at

his death Stephen prays, 'Lord Jesus receive my spirit' (Acts 7:59). The only use of the title 'Father' for God in Acts is in the opening two chapters when Jesus and then Peter speak of the Father's promise of the Spirit.

As we explore Jesus' use of the term 'Father' in his praying, we have to see – and use – the word in the light of Jesus' own words and actions. This means that we need to derive the content for the image of 'Father' from the gospel itself. In Luke's gospel Jesus speaks of and to the Father in a number of important ways, outlined below.

1 The temple as my Father's house (2:49)

The first reference to God as Father is found in the story from Jesus' childhood of the family's visit to Jerusalem (2:41–52), where Jesus stays behind in the city when the family start back to Nazareth. When Mary and Joseph eventually find Jesus in the temple, his mother asks him why he has treated them in this way. With unconscious irony he replies: 'Why were you searching for me? Did you not know that I must be in my Father's house?' (2:49).

This traditional story of Jesus' childhood reminds the reader of Jesus' continuity with the story of Israel – the covenant between God and God's people and the place of the temple as a focus of worship. More than that, it speaks of Jesus' natural, childlike and intimate relationship to God: 'the almighty Father, Creator of heaven and earth' has become simply 'my Father'. At four key points in the gospel, Jesus speaks of 'my Father', each time emphasising the trust between child and parent (10:22; 22:29; 24:49). It is clear that for Jesus, God is our true home. As Meister Eckhart wrote, 'God is at home; it is we who have gone for a walk.'[9]

2 Be compassionate as your Father is compassionate (6:36)

In Luke's so-called 'Sermon on the Plain' (6:20–49) – a much briefer collection of sayings than Matthew's 'Sermon on the Mount' – Jesus gives a series of teaching on the kingdom life, its blessings and challenges. He ends the section on loving one's enemies by saying 'Be merciful, just as your Father is merciful'

(6:36 NRSV) or 'Be compassionate as your Father is compassionate' (REB). Matthew ends the same teachings with a slightly
different emphasis: 'Be perfect, therefore, as your heavenly Father
is perfect' (Matthew 5:48). For Luke, the heart of the Father – the
central nature of God revealed by Jesus – is tender mercy and
compassion. Jesus prayed and lived out that compassionate way
and as we pray to that Compassionate One we also seek that
compassion in our own being and living.

In his teaching, Jesus does not see his relationship to God as
exclusive. 'My Father' is 'your Father'. And so he shares both the
challenge of that relationship ('Be compassionate', 'seek first the
kingdom') and the joy ('how much more ...'). He tells his disciples
not to become over-occupied or over-anxious about possessions –
food and clothes – but rather to set God's kingdom as their
overriding priority: 'Your Father knows that you need them' (i.e.
food and clothes, 12:30); 'Do not be afraid, little flock, for it is your
Father's good pleasure to give you the kingdom' (12:32). This
passionate and joyful relationship to God as child to parent cuts
through philosophical wisdom and intellectual niceties, in order to
go to the heart of our stark and total dependence on the grace and
will of God.

3 The glory of the Father (9:26; 10:21–22)

Abba, Father – my Father – speaks of Jesus' intimacy with God,
but the awesome transcendent nature of God remains. It is
expressed in the eschatological verse looking to the coming of
glory of the Son of Man (Jesus' favoured designation of himself in
the synoptic gospels): 'Those who are ashamed of me and my
words, of them the Son of Man will be ashamed when he comes in
his glory and the glory of the Father and of the holy angels' (9:26).
In this vision God's glory is shared with Jesus and the holy angels.

Jesus re-emphasises this transcendent element in his great
prayer of thanksgiving (10:21–22), a passage often called 'the
Johannine thunderbolt' because its language is more that of John's
gospel than that more customarily used in the other three gospels.
'I thank you, Father, Lord of heaven and earth ...' (10:21). It is the
one point in Luke's gospel (and Matthew's) where the relationship

of Jesus to God, son to father, is developed theologically or doctrinally. Yet even here the theological element is far less developed than in John's gospel where, for instance, Jesus says 'the Father and I are one' (John 10:30). The prayer's focus is on the Father's mysterious act of revelation – a revealing through Jesus, not to the learned and wise but to the simple, a theme echoed in Paul's description of the foolishness of the cross in 1 Corinthians 1:18–31. It is made clear here that prayer is never a controlling of God, some kind of superstitious magic, but rather a grateful openness to the mystery and majesty of God, who is beyond the grasp of our intellects, yet graciously reveals his heart.

4 Father hallowed be your name (11:2–4)

In Luke's account the teaching of the Lord's Prayer comes in response to the disciples seeing Jesus at prayer and asking him to teach them to pray. In response Jesus teaches them a prayer that reflects his own intimate and obedient relationship to God – his living out of the kingdom of God, day by day. It encourages them to turn from self to the God of grace – and to hallow God's name (the name revealed to Moses as 'I AM WHO I AM' and made known anew in Jesus), to seek God's kingdom, to recognise their daily dependence on God for sustenance, both physical and spiritual, to ask forgiveness and to accept the task of forgiving others, and to rely wholly on God to save them from the trials and temptations of life.

5 The Father who gives the Holy Spirit (11:13)

There is a strong emphasis in the gospel on the Father as Spirit-giver. It is likely that Luke and Matthew had a common source in the saying of Jesus about God giving good things (Luke 11:13; Matthew 7:11). As Matthew records the saying, Jesus said, 'How much more will the heavenly Father give good things to those who ask him' (Matthew 7:11). It is probable that Luke subtly altered the saying to emphasise that the good thing Christians should be asking for is the Holy Spirit – the energy and guiding fire of God. The Holy Spirit is a foretaste of the kingdom, so this assurance of God's gift of the Holy Spirit may link with Jesus' assurance in 12:32: 'Do not be afraid little flock, for your Father

has chosen to give you the kingdom.' The final reference to Father
in the gospel and all three references in the opening chapters of
Acts relate to the Father of promise, the one who will pour out the
Spirit into the hearts of the followers of Jesus. This universal
promise is opened up to the first disciples as they are commanded
by Jesus to stay in Jerusalem, 'to wait there for the promise of the
Father' (Acts 1:4). As the Spirit had descended on Jesus with God's
assurance, 'You are my beloved son' (3:22), so the Father sends the
Spirit to fill the disciples, to enable them to be witnesses to Jesus
and to continue Jesus' work and teaching. The Father is not a
remote figure but one who fills lives with joy and grace – the great
gift of God's own Spirit.

6 The loving father and the two sons (*15:11–32*)

For Luke, the three parables of the lost being found form a key
description of Jesus' good news. Each is important (the shepherd
and the lost sheep, the woman and the lost coin, the father and the
two sons) in describing God's joy at rescuing lost ones, but in its
subject material, human interest and narrative power the story of
the Prodigal Son stands out. The word 'father' is used nine times
and though it is made clear that this is a story about human
characters (the younger son says, 'Father, I have sinned against you
and against God …'), it is also made very clear that we are being
given a glimpse into the heart of what Jesus means by speaking of
God as Father. He is a father who gives his younger son immense
freedom to go his own way, who never gives up looking out for his
return, who runs out to embrace the returning child and tells his
older son, 'Son, you are always with me and all that is mine is
yours.' His behaviour is totally at odds with the patriarchal expectations of the society in which the story is set. He is a father who
expresses self-giving love rather than patriarchal domination. So
while the story is set in a patriarchal culture (a story of male lines of
inheritance and obligations), the father of the story transcends the
norms of the culture of his time to reach out to a son who has
become lost in his wandering from home, and then later to reach
out to the son who remained, but became equally lost in his bitter
anger and resentment. Once again compassion is at the heart of

what Jesus means by calling God 'Father': 'When the younger son was still far off, his father saw him and was filled with compassion; he ran and put his arms around him and kissed him' (15:20). The joy and compassion of the father is regarded as unjust and foolish by the elder son, who misses the heart of the matter and has in effect kept the loving father at a distance.

7 Father, your will be done (22:42)

For Jesus at Gethsemane, praying to Abba, Father, allows him to express his innermost anguish. He does not need to be polite as he asks to be spared the cup of suffering. Yet one senses that for Luke Jesus knows in his heart that it is not possible for the cup to be removed, yet prays all the same. No wonder that, according to a verse not present in some of the earliest manuscripts of Luke, 'his sweat became like great drops of blood falling down on the ground' (22:44). For Luke the cross is a harsh necessity, a mystery that at one and the same time is at odds with God's will ('this man was innocent/righteous', 23:47) and according to God's will ('was it not necessary that the Messiah should suffer these things …?' 24:26). In his masterly account of this prayer, James Resseguie describes Jesus' prayer at Gethsemane as 'the model of Christian prayer'.[10] Self-will, he says, is totally contained – enfolded – within God's will:

A   Father if you are willing
B   remove this cup from me,
B   yet, not my will
A   but yours be done.

Resseguie goes on to note: 'For Luke, the spiritual life involves both the taming of self-will and the clarifying of God's will for our lives.'[11] Praying 'Father' is deeply challenging to personal ego, yet the way of the cross – of self-giving sacrificial love – is the way of life and glory.

8 Prayers at the cross (23:34, 46)

Luke clearly has a particular emphasis to bring to his account of Jesus' crucifixion, adapting Mark's source account with material

from other sources and his own reflections. The great struggle that
is heard so brutally in the other two synoptic gospels in Jesus' cry,
'My God, my God, why have you forsaken me' ('Eloi, Eloi, lama
sabachthani', Mark 15:34), has in Luke's mind already taken place
in the garden where Jesus sweated blood in his prayer of anguish.
Now on the cross Jesus faces his death with courage and compassion. He expresses words of forgiveness towards his murderers and
words of hope to a criminal. He approaches his death with strong
words of assurance from Psalm 31:5, again using that familiar
'Father' to begin his prayer: 'Father into your hands I commit my
spirit' (23:46). In his icon of 'the Father' Luke wants to point us to
Jesus on the cross.

From these verses it becomes clear that while 'Father' is a
dominant image in the prayers of the gospel, it is one that is
moulded by the way Jesus uses and transforms this picture – as the
God of the covenant, the compassionate one, the holy one who
hears our prayers, the one who runs out to meet us, and the one
whose essence is seen on the cross. Jesus is very willing in Luke's
gospel to use images paradoxically, to overthrow the normal
expectations that surround a word. The first shall be last and the
last first; the leaders of the community are not to lord it over the
others, but to serve; the true king wears a crown of thorns. The
fact that the dispute among the disciples over who is greater is
recorded twice (9:46–48; 22:24–30) shows how important Luke
sees this lesson to be: 'The greatest among you must become like
the youngest and the leader like one who serves' (22:26).

For Luke the word 'Father' is very important but it is not sacred
in itself. Luke either does not know or chooses to omit Jesus'
prohibition of the use of the word 'Father' in addressing people
(present in Matthew 23:9). Parental (father/mother), educational
(teacher/pupil) and political (king/lord – subjects) language has
been radically transformed by Jesus. Jesus also offers other pictures
to speak of God: a shepherd seeking a lost sheep, a woman
searching for a coin, a friend tucked up in bed, and a magistrate. At
times he uses these images to illustrate, at other times to contrast
('how much more …').

As we pray – or allow the Spirit to pray within us – we meet the
same I AM whom Jesus spoke of as Abba, Father. We can be bold to

use that same word – 'Abba, Father' – recognising that its meaning is bound up with the way Jesus lived and prayed, died and was raised to life and shared the promised gift of the Spirit. But whether we use the word 'Father' or not, the relationship of intimacy, love and dependence of which it speaks is open to us all, as we open ourselves to the God shown in Jesus.

∞

Reflect and pray

God beyond all human words
be to me the embracing father.
God who shows yourself in Jesus
be to me the gift of grace.
God whose Spirit fills me daily
be to me so much more
than any words can say.

∞

Praying to Jesus

The great 'Abba' prayers give us a picture of our praying as expressing the relationship of child to parent, encouraged and opened up by the beloved child Jesus. Jesus teaches us to pray and stands alongside us as we open our hearts to the loving mystery of God.

Yet with this picture is another that grows in intensity as the gospel unfolds and comes into sharper focus in Luke's second book. It is praying not with Jesus, the teacher of prayer, but praying to Jesus, the Lord and Saviour. Throughout Luke's account terms and titles that in the Hebrew tradition would be restricted to God are applied to Jesus. He boldly uses the definite term 'the Lord' for Jesus, something the other gospel-writers are loath to do. Jesus is Son of God (1:35), Messiah and Saviour (2:11), God's beloved (3:22), the Holy one of God (4:34), the Son of Man with authority to forgive sins (5:24), God's chosen one (9:35), king (19:38) and Author of life (Acts 3:15).

In both the gospel and Acts God and Jesus are referred to as the Lord and, as the story develops, prayers are directed not only to God but to Jesus. In the gospel the boundary between conversation with Jesus and prayer to Jesus is inevitably unclear, though many of the pleas of characters in need of Jesus' help are in effect prayers. At times they are words expressing a sense of unworthiness before Jesus, the holy one of God. Peter falls on his knees before Jesus, saying: 'Go away from me, Lord, for I am a sinful man' (5:8). Likewise the centurion seeks Jesus' help for his servant, but discourages Jesus from coming to his house, sending his friends to Jesus with the message, 'Lord, do not trouble yourself, for I am not worthy to have you under my roof' (7:6). At other times the words are pleas for help. Amid the storm, the disciples wake Jesus, shouting, 'Master, master we are perishing!' (8:24). The father of the boy suffering from convulsions cries out to Jesus, 'Teacher, I beg you to look at my son; he is my only child (9:38). The ten lepers call out to Jesus: 'Jesus, Master, have mercy on us' (17:13). The penitent thief asks Jesus on the cross, 'Jesus, remember me when you come into your kingdom' (23:42). Around these pleas for help Luke creates an atmosphere of spiritual expectation and power.

In the book of Acts praying to Jesus becomes a natural action. For example, Stephen echoes Jesus' prayer on the cross ('Father, into your hands I commend my spirit') as he faces his own death, but in this situation places himself in Jesus' care: 'Lord Jesus, receive my spirit' (Acts 7:59). Later in Acts Paul has a series of conversations with Jesus, most notably on the Damascus road (Acts 9:1–9) and in the Jerusalem temple (Acts 22:17–21).

As we have noted, Jesus' own preferred term of address to God as 'Father' is not used after the first two chapters of Acts, a reminder that we need to focus on the spirit of Jesus' teaching rather than becoming fixated on particular words.

As we absorb the gospel story of Jesus and imagine ourselves present within its events it will become natural for us to pray to the main character of the story – to Jesus himself. There is nothing improper or theologically naive about doing this, though it is important that we do not limit ourselves (or God) to Jesus alone. In the gospel story Jesus always sees himself in relation to God – Abba – and to the Spirit's power.

The simplicity of talking with Jesus can be very refreshing for our praying where it has become overly formalised and polite. Ignatian spirituality highly values this intimate conversation, known as a colloquy, which often develops out of entering imaginatively into a gospel story. Yet this is not the end of the matter: not only do we pray alongside Jesus (to Abba) and to Jesus (as brother, friend, master and saviour), we are also prayed for by Jesus. The key passage relating to this is where Jesus promises that he has prayed for Peter, that Peter's denial of Jesus may not be the last word: 'Simon, Simon, listen! Satan has demanded to sift all of you like wheat, but I have prayed for you that your own faith may not fail: and you, when once you have turned back, strengthen your brothers' (22:31–32).

Jesus has prayed for Simon Peter in a very specific way – not to make Simon superhuman (the false image Simon has of himself, 'Lord, I am ready to go with you to prison and to death', 22:33), but the basic necessity that his faith may not totally fail, that he will find a path back to resurrection faith.

How and what Jesus prays for you and for me is a mystery, yet we may find a clue in Jesus' encounter with the blind beggar near Jericho (18:35–43) and his question: 'What do you want me to do for you?'

Clothed with the Holy Spirit

Luke appears to have a considerable interest in clothing for it is a recurrent theme in the account. In the stories of the demoniac and the prodigal, being re-clothed signifies a restoration of inner mind and a re-admittance into society. When Legion has been cleansed he is found sitting at the feet of Jesus (the place of a disciple), clothed and in his right mind (8:35). When the prodigal has come to his senses and has returned home his father welcomes him and calls to the servants: 'Quickly, bring out a robe – the best one – and put it on him; put a ring on his finger and sandals on his feet' (15:22).

Jesus' clothing has significance too. He enters the world naked
– wrapped by his mother in strips of swaddling cloth (2:7) – and
dies naked on a cross – his clothing divided among his execution-
ers by lots (23:34). The naked dead body is wrapped again this time
by Joseph of Arimathea and laid not now in a manger but in a rock-
hewn tomb.

Between these two events are three key moments of clothing.
Praying after his baptism, Jesus is clothed with the Holy Spirit
which 'descended upon him in bodily form like a dove' (3:22),
anointing and empowering him for the work ahead. On the
mountainside, as again Jesus is praying, God clothes him in light –
'his clothes became dazzling white' (9:29). Then in total contrast
in the dark hour of his passion Jesus is clothed in an elegant robe
provided by Herod to mock 'the king of the Jews' (23:11). Yet this
final mockery leading to the wrapping of the body in linen cloth is
not the end. In a reference reminiscent of John's gospel (though
not included in all of the oldest manuscripts) Peter enters the
empty tomb and finds the linen cloth cast to one side (24:12).
Death – and the trappings of death – has been defeated, as Jesus has
been raised and clothed in new life.

Though there are other themes linked to clothing, such as
people's anxiety, exhibitionism and injustice, the theme of restoration and new beginning echoes in Jesus' promise to his followers:
'Stay in the city until you are clothed with power from on high'
(24:49b).

The promise of this power from on high, this Holy Spirit, is not
for a special elite (the religious leaders who love their long robes
(20:46), or the rich who are so proud of their clothing, (7:25;
16:20)), but for all people. On the day of Pentecost Peter tells the
crowd that everyone who calls on the name of the Lord shall be
saved, and goes on to promise forgiveness and the gift of the Holy
Spirit to all who repent and are baptised in the name of Jesus
Christ: 'The promise is for you, for your children, and for all who
are far away, everyone whom the Lord our God calls to him' (Acts
2:39).

For Luke, the great gift of God – the great promise of Jesus – is
the Holy Spirit, the power that enables disciples of Jesus to live life
joyfully and faithfully. The Holy Spirit is fundamental to God's

work of salvation in Jesus and in the followers of Jesus. Luke refers to the Holy Spirit eighteen times in his gospel, in contrast to Mark's six references and Matthew's twelve. This despite the fact that much more will be said of the Spirit's work in his second book: Acts has fifty-seven references to the Holy Spirit. 'More than either of the other Synoptic evangelists Luke has made the Spirit an important feature of his Gospel.'[12] The Holy Spirit initiates each section of the gospel, beginning with Gabriel's promise to Mary: 'The Holy Spirit will come upon you and the power of the Most High will overshadow you; therefore the child to be born will be holy; he will be called Son of God.'

Thereafter the Holy Spirit fills Elizabeth (1:41), Zechariah (1:67) and John the Baptist (1:17, 80), descends on Jesus at his baptism as he prays (3:22), drives him into the wilderness (4:1) and back to Galilee (4:14). Jesus begins his mission declaration with the words of Isaiah, 'The Spirit of the Lord is upon me' (4:18). As the seventy-two return from their mission Jesus rejoices in the Holy Spirit and gives thanks to God. Setting his face to Jerusalem he begins to speak of the importance of the Holy Spirit (11:13; 12:10–12).

Both Matthew and Luke record Jesus' teaching about the need to ask, seek and knock and the promise that the Father will give. However, as we have noted already, while Matthew ends the passage with the words, 'How much more will the heavenly Father give good things to those who ask him' (Matthew 7:11), Luke changes 'good things' to the 'Holy Spirit' (11:13). Just as the disciples are to seek one thing – the kingdom – and not to be anxious about many things (clothing, food, etc.) so they are to ask for one thing – the Holy Spirit. That is the one gift needed for life. As John the Baptist had said, Jesus is 'the one who will baptise with the Holy Spirit and fire' (3:16). As the gospel draws to a close Jesus tells his friends to stay in the city: 'See I am sending upon you what the Father promised: so stay here in the city until you have been clothed with power from on high' (24:49).

The promised power, the Holy Spirit, is in Luke's eyes very much the Spirit of Jesus (Acts 16:6–7), enabling the activity and teaching of Jesus begun in the gospel (Acts 1:1) to be continued in the life of the disciples, the followers of the Way, both individually

and as a community. 'The same Spirit which inspired and empow-
ered him, inspires and empowers them: so much so, that it is
understood as the Spirit of Jesus himself.'[13] The Holy Spirit is the
Father's greatest gift and its coming a sign of God's love and
goodness (11:13) and the trustworthiness and truth of God's
promises (24:49; Acts 2:11). The Holy Spirit binds the community
(male and female, young and old and, in time, Jew and Gentile)
together as one and enables the followers of Jesus to communicate
God's acts of power (Acts 2:12), giving them the words to say
(12:12), the boldness to say them (Acts 4:31) and bringing about
signs and wonders (Acts 2:43; 8:13). The Spirit brings about
prophetic words and visions (Acts 2:17–21; 11:28) and speaking in
tongues (Acts 19:6), calling individuals to particular work (Acts
13:2) and guiding them in that work step by step (Acts 16:6–7).
The Spirit stirs up joy in the disciples (Acts 13:52) as in Jesus
(10:21). The event of Jesus and his exaltation releases the Spirit in a
dramatic and potentially universal way, but this is not to dismiss the
work of the Spirit in previous generations and in particular in the
story of Israel (Acts 4:25; 28:25).

So the free Spirit of God flows through the story of humanity,
the story of Israel, the story of Jesus and of his continued work in
and through his followers. The Spirit is not simply the great gift to
be prayed for but is the key to our praying, nudging us forward to
the embrace of God, encouraging us to persist, bringing us to our
senses, lifting our hearts in joy and praise, opening our eyes to the
needs around us and empowering us to play our part in the
continuing work of Jesus.

∞

**Clothe us with your Spirit,
clothe us with your power;
power made known in weakness;
power that's shown in love.**

∞

The silence and the voice of God

If the importance of a character was to be judged by the amount of speech given to that character, there would be no doubt of Jesus' importance in Luke's gospel. Peter might be regarded as of some importance (with a series of brief lines), alongside Pharisees of unknown names. Women are found to be largely silent, apart from the early words of Mary and Elizabeth, the short outburst by Martha and the blessings offered by a few unknown women. But then most of the (male) apostles and the other disciples who gather around Jesus have no speaking parts. More importantly God is largely silent with only two key moments of divine speech in the gospel (echoed by two more in Acts). Of course God has his messengers (the angel Gabriel and others) and supremely the one sent (Jesus himself) but the gospel-writer does not lightly include the voice from heaven. The two key moments in the gospel are at the baptism of Jesus (3:22) and at the transfiguration (9:35), both occasions when Luke emphasises that Jesus was praying. The two key moments in Acts are the vision of Peter where the voice from heaven says, 'It is not for you to call profane what God counts clean' (Acts 10:15), and on the Damascus road when the voice is now identified with Jesus, 'Saul, Saul, why are you persecuting me?' (Acts 9:4; 22:7; 26:14). Here the visionary encounter is with Jesus as it is in a later experience while Paul is held in prison in Jerusalem (Acts 23:11).

Within Luke's account, God remains a mystery wrapped in cloud and silence, yet visible and vocal in the life of Jesus and in the life of all who follow the Jesus way through the Spirit's work. The Spirit is a physical manifestation of God's presence and power (in dove, wind and fire, and in the signs and wonders shown by those who come under the Spirit's influence).

The only other point where God speaks directly is in a parable Jesus tells of a rich man who lives life as if it were a closed system made up only of his own plans and prosperity. At the moment when the man decides to build a bigger barn and take life easy God speaks: 'You fool! This very night your life is being demanded of you. And the things you have prepared, whose will they be?' (12:20).

Otherwise the presence of God is a silent one – a cloud both to signify faithful presence and ultimate mystery. We are reminded that all words ultimately fall short in the face of what in Whittier's famous words is 'the silence of eternity interpreted by love'.[14] This silence of God throws the gospel-hearer back to the words of Jesus and to the Spirit's guiding power. It is interesting that in the parable of the Pharisee and tax collector, no interruption from heaven takes place within the story, unlike the parable of the rich man with his barns. The Pharisee continues his pseudo prayer, which degenerates into self-deception, pride and contempt for others. The tax collector's simple prayer, 'God be merciful to me a sinner', is heard, but the story does not tell us how the tax collector comes to know that it has been heard. There is silence. Only Jesus adds the comment, 'I tell you this man went down to his house justified rather than the other' (18:14). The silence can all too easily be filled up with our own voice – telling us perhaps what we want to hear or wallowing in our own wretchedness. Yet, by God's grace and with the Spirit's help, that silence can lead us to an inner listening for the voice of Christ. God's word to Jesus at his baptism is of affirming love and delight: 'You are my son, the beloved; with whom I am well pleased' (3:22). God's other word in the gospel – at the transfiguration – is to the disciples, again affirming Jesus: 'This is my son, my chosen' (9:35), but adding the key phrase, 'Listen to him.'

∞

Great Love,
silence
my chattering tongue
my restless body
my distracted mind
my anxious heart
and in your silence
recreate me.

∞

Prayer and community

The prayer relationship expressed in Jesus' praying and teaching is intensely personal and intimate, but far from individualistic. Jesus withdraws to remote places to focus and reflect, but is not separated from his followers or from the wider community by this intensity of concentration. He teaches his followers to pray simply 'Father' (rather than the more corporate 'our Father' of Matthew's gospel). But the prayer itself is very much a community prayer: 'Give *us* today our daily bread'; 'forgive *our* sins'; 'do not bring *us* to the test'. Similarly when Jesus calls his disciples to be alert and pray he addresses them as a group rather than individually (22:40, 46). When we move to the second part of Luke's story – the mission of Jesus' disciples to be witnesses to all nations beginning in Jerusalem – we find the main picture of prayer is of the followers gathering to pray together. As he explores the spirituality of Luke-Acts, Stephen Barton notes that 'prayer has a strong, horizontal, and corporate dimension'.[15] The apostles meet in the upstairs room in Jerusalem and 'with one accord were constantly at prayer, together with a group of women, and Mary, the mother of Jesus and his brothers' (Acts 1:14). It is when all are gathered that the Spirit comes, and Luke emphasises that the Spirit comes on them all, men and women, young and old, so fulfilling the prophecy of Joel as Peter makes clear in his speech: 'For the promise is for you, for your children, and for all who are far away, everyone whom the Lord our God calls to him' (Acts 2:39). As the story of Acts unfolds it becomes clear that this inclusive vision is to include Jew and Gentile, to form a new redeemed community.

When new disciples join the group they too gather for prayer: 'The believers met constantly to hear the apostles teach, and to share the common life, to break bread and to pray' (Acts 2:42). The context of prayer for the first disciples is overwhelmingly communal, a shared action, but this does not exclude individuals from praying alone. Peter goes up on to the house roof to pray at noon and is there confronted with a vision and with God's inner voice (Acts 10:9–16).

In this way Luke holds together personal and corporate prayer: 'the spirituality of Luke is certainly personal, but it is not privatized: it is a matter of concern to individuals, but it is not individualistic.'[16] Eduard Schweizer sees this holding together of individual experiences and church context as 'one of the most important contributions Luke made to the New Testament'.[17] Praying detached from the community is liable to become individualistic and feeble, but equally community prayer without a personal dimension can become closed to God's intimacy and personal call. The two need to be held together, both when we pray alone and in company: the prayers of the community need opportunities for personal prayer and the prayers of individuals need to have times when the person's incorporation in the wider community of faith can be affirmed and celebrated.

Of course one of the challenges of the community dimension of prayer is the imperfect nature of the community, and the individuals that make it up. Luke gives a somewhat idealised picture of community in the immediate aftermath of the Pentecost event (Acts 2:41–47; 4:32–37), but recognises that this deep fellowship is not the whole picture. Before the event (during the public ministry of Jesus) the disciples are shown to be all too fallible and often concerned with their own status and position in the group. After the initial flame of Pentecost, weaknesses and failings again surface in the community: the failure to share – shown with grim drama in the story of Ananias and Sapphira (Acts 5:1–11), the neglect of Hellenist widows and the ensuing complaints (Acts 6:1), the struggle to work out leadership roles (Acts 6:2–7), the challenge of persecution (Acts 8:1) after the initial favourable response of the surrounding community (Acts 2:47), the dissention over the inclusion of Gentiles (Acts 15:1–2), the disagreement of Paul and Barnabas over Mark's failure (Acts 15:36–39), and Paul's warning of difficulties ahead to the church at Ephesus (Acts 20:30–31). Even when Spirit-filled, the human and fallible nature of the Church remains. Yet far from encouraging us to withdraw from fellowship with other Christians, this very fallibility should encourage us to draw closer to each other. The living out of Christian community – in worship and service – will be the place where we learn that 'the greatest must become like the youngest and the leader like one who serves' (Luke 22:24–28; 9:46–48).

Praying with the people of Israel

In Luke's account the disciples ask Jesus to teach them to pray, as John the Baptist taught his disciples, implying a new way of praying in the light of Jesus and in response to seeing Jesus pray. However, the way of prayer Jesus teaches and demonstrates is deeply rooted in the prayer of Israel. As we have seen, Jesus' favoured form of address of God as 'Father' reflects the covenant tradition of his people and the image of God's parenting of the beloved but stubborn child, Israel (as, for example, in Jeremiah and Hosea). While Jesus brings new depth and intimacy to the prayer form, he also clearly sees himself standing in line with the prophets and teachers of the Hebrew Scriptures. Luke emphasises the continuity with the prayers of Israel in many ways. The great canticles in the early chapters show the psalm tradition to be alive within the new Christian community. New hymns of thanksgiving have been produced echoing the songs of Israel, in the context of the Christ event.

The first great song is placed on the lips of Mary, in response to her experience of being drawn into God's work of salvation. Her response to Gabriel, 'Here I am, the servant of the Lord; let it be with me according to your word' (1:38), is given as the great example of human response to divine word and action, a pattern to be taken up and followed by the rest of the church community. Luke purposely identifies Mary and other members of Jesus' family as being with the apostles in the upper room in Jerusalem, praying together between the ascension of Jesus and the coming of the Holy Spirit at Pentecost.

Luke also values highly the Jerusalem temple as a place of prayer, all the more poignant as he may well have written the gospel soon after the destruction of the temple. Jerusalem is the place from which the gospel is taken out first to Judaea, Samaria and to the farthest corners of the earth (Acts 1:8). Though the story of Acts moves steadily towards Rome, symbolic of the nations, and the gospel comes to be preached more to Gentiles than Jews, it remains a story founded on the law and the prophets, fulfilled in the man of Galilee and offered to Jew and Gentile alike. The key forms of prayer in Luke's account – exultant praise, petition and lament – again reflect the forms of prayer to be found in the Psalms. In fact Jesus' prayer on the cross as he approaches death is a verse from Psalm 31, adapted with Jesus' characteristic way of addressing God: 'Father, into your hands, I commit my spirit' (23:46).

The increasing emphasis on the mission to the Gentiles is not a rejection of God's people, Israel, but a challenge to more of God's people to recognise the claims of Jesus. At the end of Acts Paul quotes from Isaiah about looking but not seeing, hearing but not understanding (Acts 28:26, 27) in the same way as Jesus did when speaking of his parables (8:10). Both uses of the quotation are there not to describe an inevitable status quo, but to challenge listeners to respond. For Luke, Jesus remains the hope of Israel; the inclusion of the Gentiles – those who are far away – in this hope is an extraordinary act of God that should evoke joy and praise.

Accompanied by angels

In a glorious book of poetry on the theme of the incarnation Lucy Shaw points out that in his birth and resurrection Jesus was 'accompanied by angels'.[18] The phrase echoes that used by St Clement of Alexandria when he wrote, 'Even when a person prays alone he is accompanied by angels.'[19]

Of course within first-century Judaism there were different beliefs about angels, as there are within twenty-first-century Christianity. The Sadducees rejected any belief in angels, seeing it as threatening the autonomy of human beings, while the Pharisees considered there to be a variety of spiritual beings including angels and demons.

Belief in angels seems to be making a comeback in Western Christianity (and New Age religions) after years of neglect, but there are still many who feel that including this belief is an unnecessary distraction. However, it is worth recognising the part played within the gospel by the angels or messengers of God. The distinction between angels and human beings is at times blurred. Jesus says that after the resurrection people are like angels and do not marry (20:36). And in Acts, as he addresses the Jerusalem

Council, Stephen is described as having 'the face of an angel' (Acts 6:15). In Acts 12 Peter assumes that the angel's intervention in opening the jail door is simply a vision and only when he finds himself outside on the city streets does he recognise it as real! There is certainly no necessity to regard angels as having wings. The messengers of the resurrection who greet the women at the tomb are described as two men in dazzling garments, who suddenly appear, ask the women 'Why are you looking among the dead for one who is alive?' and tell them to remember the words of Jesus (24:4–7). Angels have a similar role as messengers at the beginning of the gospel, announcing God's action first to Zechariah, then to Mary and later to the shepherds. Their appearance may terrify those to whom they bring their message, but each time they tell their hearers not to be afraid. As Jim Forest comments, 'angels are associated with our overcoming of all those paralyzing fears which prevent each of us from living a God-centred life.'[20]

Between the birth of Jesus and his resurrection angels appear only within Jesus' stories and teaching. The one exception is in the garden of Gethsemane: 'Then an angel from heaven appeared to him and gave him strength' (22:43). Scholars are divided as to whether the verse was in Luke's original manuscript. As Joseph Fitzmyer notes, 'the matter is hotly debated among textual critics today'.[21] He himself omits the verse from his translation, but there are some good reasons for including it. Luke omits the reference in Matthew and Mark to angels ministering to Jesus in the wilderness after his time of temptation and instead ends that story with the chilling words that Satan left Jesus 'biding his time' (4:13). Omitting the reference to the angels' help at that point makes its inclusion at the ultimate test at Gethsemane all the more telling. It is a powerful picture of encouragement and strengthening and one that could be valuable for us.

However, the dominant picture of angels within Luke's story is one of joy and praise. At the birth of Christ the angels sing before the shepherds, 'Glory to God in the highest heaven and on earth peace among those whom God favours' (2:14). As Paul Borgmann notes, 'The angels have offered a two-line summary of good news that encompasses not only what salvation looks like, but *for whom* such salvation is intended and *by whom*.'[22] In Luke 15 Jesus describes the joy of the angels over the one sinner who repents. Heaven is not a lonely, silent, abstract place, but one full of laughter, celebration and praise. 'Joy is not confined to earth alone.'[23] As we pray, alone or with others, we can ask the Spirit to use our imagination to connect us to this eternal song and touch this divine joy.

Prayer as struggle

Prayer described in Luke's gospel is far from a comfortable exercise. Yes, it can involve great joy, but also deep lament; there is thanksgiving and affirmation, but also wrestling and questioning; the Spirit can comfort, but it can also disturb. So it is that the first recorded time of prayer in the wilderness for Jesus immediately after his baptism, though initiated by the Spirit, becomes a battle royal between self-interest and God-interest, between the tempter and the Son of God, between the false way and the good way (4:1–12): 'If you are the Son of God' is repeated three times as the devil takes Jesus from the wilderness (the place of Israel's testing) to a view of the nations (the place of power and domination) to Jerusalem (the place of Jesus' final testing).

For Luke the forty days in the wilderness is a precursor to the deeper trial Jesus will face in the garden of Gethsemane – the place where he will again align himself with the will of his Father despite the cost involved: 'Father, if you are willing, remove this cup from me; yet, not my will but yours be done' (22:42).

In the wilderness, the place of testing, Jesus refuses to succumb to the simplistic solution (stones into bread), the way of self-promoting power and glory (worshipping the devil), and the distorted use of Scripture to test God's care (jumping from the temple pinnacle). A false way of magic, power and safety is placed before Jesus, who rejects it for a way of self-giving, service and risk-filled compassion.

Between those two key points of struggle and testing Luke makes clear that Jesus is willing to give extended time to prayer, to discern the next step in his mission and journey. He describes Jesus spending the whole night in prayer to God before choosing the twelve from among his disciples (6:12). The implication is that prayer is not a simplistic short cut to discerning God's will, not a complacent communion, but a deeply testing action. Borgmann notes that for Luke prayer is essential, not peripheral: 'Such difficult times require prayer for one's strength, not pointing to magic "escape" possibilities.'[24]

The awesome wrestling Jesus undertakes in his praying puts into perspective our own challenges in prayer. However, our struggle may not be within prayer, but a struggle to begin. Luke sees Jesus as providing a school in prayer as the disciples see him pray and ask him, 'Lord teach us to pray, as John taught his disciples' (11:1). Jesus then gives them a simple model of prayer – the 'Father' prayer (a simpler version of the Lord's Prayer than in Matthew's gospel). He encourages his followers simply to ask God to help them pray, as a small child asks a parent for food or a friend asks to borrow bread or a plaintiff demands justice. Fundamental is a recognition of need – a loosening of our instinct for independence, self-sufficiency or complacency. Thus the tax collector's prayer, for all the discomfort the tax collector feels (uncomfortable in the temple precincts, standing afar and overawed by God not raising his eyes to heaven), is heard while the Pharisee speaks only to himself (18:9–14). It is a triumph of content over form, sincerity and simplicity over self-centredness and sophistication.

It is likely that as we 'progress in the spiritual life', or rather think that we do, we again and again need to become beginners asking 'Lord, teach us to pray.' Simon Tugwell speaks of 'this elusiveness of prayer, this systematic impossibility of really knowing how to do it' as 'an integral part of the scriptural view of prayer'.[25] Again and again we will need to ask the Spirit to stir us from complacency (or despair) and to return us to that persistent determined prayer that Jesus describes in his parables (11:5–13; 18:1–8), that alertness and strength required for the kingdom life (21:34–36). Luke recognises the struggle but sees in Jesus the encouragement we need 'to pray always and not to lose heart' (18:1).

Prayer as reorientation

The Gospel, the kingdom message and action of Jesus, is deeply challenging of the status quo, be this economic, political or religious. The economic status quo ('the rich man in his castle, the poor man at the gate') is challenged by Jesus' teaching on possessions. The widow in her sacrificial gift gives more than all the rich (21:1–4); Lazarus will be comforted by God, the rich man condemned (16:19–31). 'Blessed are the poor' (6:20), 'woe to the rich' (6: 24); God 'has filled the hungry with good things and sent the rich away empty' (1:53). In the face of this challenge some like Zacchaeus respond, while others like the rich young ruler turn away in sadness or anger.

The political status quo is challenged by Jesus' new way of seeing power. He tells his disciples that among the Gentiles kings lord it over their subjects, but not so for the disciples, 'rather the greatest among you must become like the youngest and the leader like one who serves' (22:26). The power of the emperor and the governor is put into perspective by the birth of a child placed in a manger. Again in Mary's great song of divine revolution she celebrates that God 'has brought down the powerful from their thrones and lifted up the lowly' (1:52). Herod and Pilate are shown to be powerless as Jesus faces the cross. The unjust judge is shown to be weak in the face of the widow's persistent prayer. The governor Felix feels threatened by the words of Paul who is in chains. The reaction to Jesus is again a divided one, leading ultimately to the cross where many soldiers mock Jesus, but one centurion declares him innocent and righteous.

The religious status quo is challenged again and again by Jesus' words and actions. The structures of tithing, Sabbath keeping, rules of clean and unclean food are put into question. The holy temple itself is condemned as a 'den of robbers' and reclaimed as a place of prayer and teaching. Jesus' parables turn the world upside down, with a Pharisee who tithes being found wrong with God, while a tax collector who simply asks for mercy being right with God (18:10–14).

No wonder the key theme of Jesus' teaching, and the teaching of his followers is that of repentance. The world's framework of power, wealth and religion has been overthrown and now a new way is being offered. The mob in Thessalonica accuses Paul and his companions of being people 'who have turned the world upside down' (Acts 17:6). Jesus' message is a challenge to repent, turn round and enter this way of life, this new kingdom.

Walter Brueggemann's study of the Psalms sheds light on this dynamic of repentance and new life. Drawing on the work of Paul Ricoeur, he categorises the psalms as prayers of orientation, disorientation and reorientation. Following this terminology the gospel is in essence reorientation – the startling action of God in Christ transforming reality, the kingdom of God breaking into the world order. The characteristic response to such reorientation is celebration. Brueggemann gives the three celebrations in Luke 15 as examples of how such 'reversals must be celebrated'.[26] Yet there is also at times resistance – a wish to hold on to the old order. The reorientation does not come about by one's own efforts; it is God's surprising and gracious work, but it does require us to accept what God has done. That in effect is the place of repentance. Repentance is necessary repeatedly – a conscious returning to God, a conscious seeking of God's kingdom and will. 'If any want to become my followers, let them deny themselves and take up their cross daily and follow me' (9:23). Luke emphasises this by his addition of the word 'daily' in this saying (compared to Mark and Matthew) to stress that this act of turning round is not a one-off event, but an act to be repeated again and again in our lives.

Prayer as lament

The characteristic and dominant note in the gospel is joy, but it is not unqualified joy. Luke recognises the strange pathos of reality, the joy and anguish of life. Paul Borgmann speaks of Luke's message as being one of 'a difficult joy, and a strange peace', and goes on to note that 'there is a dark side to the good news, an inevitable disruption'.[27] Elements of what Brueggmann describes as disorientation are to be found in the gospel, giving rise to lament – an outpouring of grief, questions and complaint before God. Lament centres on five events:

- People's mixed responses to Jesus and in particular the division within the people of Israel between those who

accept and those who reject Jesus: 'This child is destined
for the falling and rising of many in Israel, and to be a sign
that will be opposed' (2:34). Luke is clear that Jesus has
come to bring peace, shalom, to the world, but ironically
this Gospel of peace divides people in their response. Jesus
speaks of this division in families and households in fierce
and ironic terms that are best understood as lament
(12:49–53).

- The future destruction of Jerusalem and the temple: this
  forms the focus of Jesus' own lamentation, more painful
  to him in some ways than his own rejection. As Jesus sees
  Jerusalem he weeps over it: 'If you, even you, had only
  recognised the things that make for peace! But now they
  are hidden from your eyes. Indeed the days will come
  upon you when your enemies will set up ramparts around
  you and surround you, and hem you in on every side'
  (19:42, 43). When the women of Jerusalem weep, as Jesus
  is dragged to the cross, Jesus tells them not to weep for
  him but for themselves and their children, ending with
  words of foreboding: 'If they do this when the wood is
  green, what will happen with it is dry?' (23:31).

- The suffering and death of Jesus, the culmination of his
  rejection: in the face of this the disciples are bewildered.
  On the road to Emmaus two friends voice their bewilder-
  ment before Jesus – the hidden stranger who is walking
  beside them asking them what has been happening: 'The
  things about Jesus of Nazareth, who was a prophet mighty
  in deed and word before God and all the people, and how
  our chief priests and leaders handed him over to be
  condemned to death and crucified him. But we had
  hoped he was the one to redeem Israel' (24:19–21). Peter
  draws on this element of lament in his preaching when he
  speaks of 'this Jesus whom you crucified' (Acts 2:36), and
  Luke describes how the crowd were 'cut to the heart'
  (Acts 2:37). Though Luke sees the crucifixion as part of
  God's definite plan, as Peter announces in his Pentecost
  speech (Acts 2:23), this does not diminish the sense of
  horror and grief at the killing of the Messiah.

- The persecution of the followers of Jesus: in the gospel Jesus tells of persecutions to come (21:12) and in Acts this becomes focused in a special way in the story of Stephen, the first martyr, but then repeated in the stories of all the first disciples and carried on in the story of Paul. Luke writes that the stoning of Stephen started a severe persecution of the Church (Acts 8:1). The Church is scattered and ravaged, though this very scattering becomes a way in which the gospel seed is spread. Yet the pain of persecution and loss remains: 'devout men buried Stephen and made loud lamentation over him' (Acts 8:2).
- The delayed fulfilment of God's kingdom, manifest in Jesus: this is echoed in the repeated calls for persistence, strength and courage in prayer. The book of Acts begins with the disciples questioning Jesus about the future and Jesus replying, 'It is not for you to know the times or periods that the Father has set by his own authority' (Acts 1:7).

Luke recognises that he and his readers live in in-between times. They live in the now of the kingdom (following the coming of Jesus and his continued work through the Holy Spirit) and the not yet of the kingdom (the fulfilment of God's shalom and the return of Jesus in glory). Luke and Jesus himself recognise the tension of this now and not yet. Will the kingdom come? Is God's justice to be permanently frustrated? Does God care? Luke's answer is that prayer must be persistent, even if the kingdom is slow to come. The kingdom's fulfilment is in the future, but God will give the Holy Spirit to enable his disciples to live in these in-between times. It is surely no accident that Jesus gives three parables, or examples, to encourage persistence in prayer that liken the hearer of the request to a sleepy friend (11:5–8), a bad father (11:11–13) and an unjust judge (18:1–8). Hidden within these stories there seem to be ordinary peoples' laments or complaints at God. Is God – who calls himself our friend – asleep behind locked doors, deaf to our needs? Is God – who calls himself our father – a bad father tricking us with scorpions when we ask for fish? Is God – who calls himself our judge – an unjust judge, who refuses to hear our plea for justice. These stories of Jesus give hearers permission to voice their frustration with God, their own doubts and confusions, but at the same time lead them forward to know the depth and breadth of God's love. Each time Jesus contrasts the reality of God – the true friend, the loving parent, the just one – with these human distortions, but he recognises that prayer raises these issues. Does God hear the cry of his people? The grace of God – shown in the Gospel of peace, the victory of the resurrection, the spreading of the message of repentance and forgiveness from Jerusalem to all nations and the gift of the Holy Spirit – allows the disciples of Jesus again and again to move from lament to joy. That gracious movement does not deny the place of lament; in fact it requires it as part of the faith journey and the transforming work of God. The dynamic remains not simply in the story of Luke-Acts, but in our own times too.

Prayer as celebration

Joy is a key note in Luke's gospel. H. J. Cadbury comments that 'there is a triumphant joy about Luke's story'.[28] Repeatedly the events surrounding Jesus evoke a response of joy and praise among the ordinary people (as opposed to those with status to lose). It is as if Luke's narrative is paused repeatedly to call people to rejoice and worship, to invite them to be lost in 'wonder, love and praise'[29] as the gospel impacts on them; 'the motif of joy and rejoicing is all pervasive'.[30] William Morrice notes 53 references to joy in Luke's gospel and a further 24 in Acts. 'Thus 24% of the New Testament vocabulary for joy is contained in the writings of Luke.'[31] Mark's gospel by contrast has very few references to joy at all, making Luke's focus all the more significant. 'It is Luke's Gospel that is *par excellence* "the Gospel of Joy"'.[32] As Jesus rides into Jerusalem 'the whole company of his disciples in their joy began to sing aloud the praises of God for all the great things they had seen' (19:37). Joy cannot be suppressed or kept down, it has to be expressed in praise of God. When some Pharisees tell Jesus to restrain his disciples, to silence their songs of praise (19:39), Jesus answers, 'I tell you if my disciples are silent, the stones will shout aloud' (19:40). So creation itself (the very stones) is caught up in joy and praise.

More than this, the human joy and praise that recurs repeatedly through the story of Jesus' ministry echoes the joy and praise of heaven, among the angels of God. There is heavenly joy over the return of one lost one to God's embrace (15:5, 7, 10, 32), and the song of the angels – glory to God and on earth peace (2:14) – is echoed by the disciples' song (peace in heaven, glory in highest heaven, 19:38). The gospel begins with the angels bringing news of great joy and ends with the disciples returning to Jerusalem full of joy (24:52). The theme of joy continues in Acts as the disciples are filled with joy and the Holy Spirit. Despite the real opposition and persecution the early Christian community experiences through the story of Acts, the note of thankfulness and praise remains. At the beginning of the gospel, Mary voices this joy and praise in the great Magnificat song: 'My soul proclaims the greatness of the Lord, and my spirit rejoices in God my saviour.'

Prayer will involve struggle, repentance and lament and will require courage, persistence and humility, but it cannot rest within this sphere alone. It must open out into joyful praise of the one who has done great things, is doing great things here and now and will do great things in the time to come. The French poet Leon Bloy commented, 'Joy is the most infallible sign of the presence of God.'[33] Quoting a phrase of William Wordsworth C. S. Lewis entitled the story of his early years leading up to his conversion 'Surprised by Joy'. Interestingly he ends by saying that joy is a sign rather than the key: 'It was valuable only as a pointer to something other and outer.'[34] An anxious search for joy is self-defeating; joy by its nature is a gift and a grace.

Seeking God's kingdom

Not all the prayers within the gospel are healthy or positive. There are subtle warnings that human praying can be infected with that egoism, self-centredness and self-deception that are the great human failings. The classic parable to illustrate this is the parable of the Pharisee and the tax collector. The Pharisee prays, 'God I thank you that I am not like other people, thieves, rogues, adulterers, or even like this tax collector. I fast twice a week; and give a tenth of all my income' (18:11,12).

One could imagine that the Pharisee of the parable continued in that vein for a lot longer, battering God with his pompous self-righteousness until eventually he degenerates into a list of his own achievements and merits. This prayer soon ceases to be addressed to God and becomes a way of talking to and bolstering oneself. Jesus says that this man does not go home right with God. Luke comments that the parable is aimed at those who are sure of their own goodness and look down on everyone else. In other words the prayer is at fault not only in its arrogance before the holy God, its self-righteous self-centredness, but in the attitude it contains towards other people. Prayer is never simply a matter of 'me and my God'; it is bound up with our lives, actions and attitudes, and the challenge to live the kingdom way.

The choice presented in the gospel is very stark: a house built on rock to represent those who act on Jesus' words and a house built on sand to represent those who do not. Jesus protests, 'Why do you call me Lord, Lord and do not do what I tell you?' (6.46). Prayers as words, however noble, are flawed without being bound up with action. In Luke's account, love for God and love for neighbour are not two commands as in Matthew's gospel; they are bound together, as one answer to how to live and inherit eternal life. 'You shall love the Lord your God with all your heart, and with all your soul and with all your strength, and with all your mind; and your neighbour as yourself' (10:27). Interestingly, in Luke's version, that synthesis of love for God and neighbour is given not by Jesus (as in Matthew and Mark), but by the lawyer who comes with the question itself. It is then in exploring the lawyer's second question, 'Who is my neighbour?' that Jesus gives the greater challenge through the parable of the Good Samaritan. Some have read this parable as exalting action over prayer, seeing the priest and the scribe as being preoccupied with their religious duties rather than in compassion for the stranger. Of course no explanation is given for the priest's and scribe's actions, or lack of action, but certainly in all our thinking about prayer, love for God and love for neighbour must be bound together; reflection and action go hand in hand.

That the two are inextricably linked together is re-emphasised when Jesus accuses the Pharisees of being concerned with the minutia of the law and neglecting 'justice and the love of God' (11:42). As a liberation theologian, Jon Sobrino emphasises the place of action in the heart of our praying, outlining a threefold structure of prayer in 'hearing the word of God, doing the word listened to, and responding with thanksgiving or a request for forgiveness',[35] depending on the deed. 'This' he continues 'is the place to utter "Abba" either as Jesus did in giving thanks, or as the prodigal son did in asking for forgiveness.'[36]

More than this, Jesus sees our picture of neighbour as being crucial to our vision of God. The focus in the encounter with the lawyer is not on the love for God, for Jesus can assume that the lawyer knows what that means, at least in theory. Rather it is on 'Who is my neighbour?' Unless that is answered correctly, love for God will be a sham. Distorted or narrowed views of neighbour – according to race, religion, gender, sexuality, age, ability or background – will twist our vision of God. True love for neighbour and true love for God are woven together. This extends to those we term enemies. 'But I say to you that listen, love your enemies, do good to those who hate you, bless those who curse you, pray for those who abuse you' (6:27). Jesus continues to bind together our relationship to God and relationship to others in a whole series of passages: 'Be merciful, just as your Father is merciful' (6:36); 'Do not judge and you will not be judged; do not condemn and you will not be condemned. Forgive and you will be forgiven; give, and it will be given to you' (6:37, 38); 'Whoever welcomes this child in my name welcomes me and whoever welcomes me welcomes the one who sent me' (9:48). He teaches his disciples to pray 'Father ... forgive us our sins for we forgive everyone indebted to us' (11:4).

Salvation comes to Zacchaeus' home both when he welcomes Jesus and when he commits himself to reach out to the poor and to those he has defrauded. When Michael Campbell-Johnston reflected on prayer he recalled how a fellow Jesuit was asked to choose 'two gospel passages that spoke to him best about prayer'. He picked Luke 11:1–4, 'Lord teach us to pray' (the Lord's Prayer) and Luke 10:25–37, 'Who is my neighbour?' (the parable of the Good Samaritan). He considered them as two aspects of the one action, our relationship to our creator and saviour, whose purpose is good. He concluded: 'Prayer "does" this to us – makes us contemplative and compassionate neighbours to the world as it is, in order to make the world what God intended.'[37]

At the heart of the action that arises from prayer is the seeking of God's kingdom, God's liberating rule over all of life. So Jesus teaches his disciples to recognise the kingdom in their midst (17:21; 21:31), to seek the kingdom above all else (12:31) and to pray for God's kingdom to come. This kingdom is about true peace and justice – restored relationships between people and with God. Justice and the dangers of riches and possessions are recurring themes in the gospel. The story of Lazarus puts in sharp relief injustices and inequalities of society, and the passionate anger of God at such wrongs (16:19–31). The rich young ruler refuses Jesus' challenge to let go possessions, give to the poor and follow him. This gives rise to Jesus' comment about how hard it is for those with wealth to enter the kingdom of God (18:24), echoing the parable of the rich fool (12:13–34). Thankfully what is impossible for mortals is possible for God and the grace of God enables the rich (and probably dishonestly rich) Zacchaeus to welcome Jesus and receive salvation. The sign that this has taken place is that he acts to give to the poor and reimburse those he has defrauded. His new relationship to Jesus has inevitable consequences for his relationship to society and to his neighbours.

Luke gives a glimpse of the kingdom in operation in the early moments of the new Christian community when it has been filled with the Spirit. This is a community where all, whatever their background, gather in homes to eat food together with 'glad and generous hearts, praising God and having the good will of all the people' (Acts 2:46–47). Luke notes the common ownership among Christians in Acts 2:44 and 4:32: 'All who believed were together and had all things in common; they would sell their possessions and goods and distribute the proceeds to all, as any had need.'

This vision fades to some extent later in Acts, under the pressure of internal failings, external persecution and scattering and the sheer scale of the growing Church. However, it is the influence of this vision of mutual responsibility that has Paul take up a collection for the Jerusalem church at a time of famine. He tells the elders from Ephesus of the importance of supporting the weak, 'remembering the words of the Lord Jesus, for he himself said, "It is more blessed to give than to receive" ' (Acts 20:35), words attributed to Jesus that are found only in Acts.

∞

Lord, may my words be few,
my every action true,
my hope fixed on you.

∞

God's embrace

We have been trained to analyse, organise, dissect, manipulate and control the reality that we see around us. Yet these tools that are so useful in many areas of life (from scientific research to cake baking) serve us poorly in our relationships to other people, let alone to the divine mystery that created us. Treating everything as an object degrades life. If prayer is the attempt to manipulate and control an object – getting God to do what we want – it will fail. If prayer is a relationship then all kinds of possibilities develop. The aim ceases to be getting God to do something for us; the aim becomes conversation and embrace.

The great parable of the father and the two sons speaks of this journey from seeing God as an object (an *I–It* relationship in Martin Buber's thinking), to God as a subject (an *I–Thou* relationship); 'The primary word *I–Thou* establishes the world of relation.'[38] The younger son begins by regarding his father as a provider of money, otherwise disposable and irrelevant to his big journey and big plans. Only in the company of the pigs does the son come to his senses. Some kind of relationship to his father would be better than that: 'Treat me as one of your hired servants' (15:19). As the son makes that move and returns home, his father runs out to meet him. The embrace is the moment of extreme grace in the story expressing acceptance, forgiveness, longing and love. This is the joy of God in me – and in you – as we journey back. It is pure grace, but grace that respects our human freedom to go our own way. The silent embrace, the divine kiss – these are the heights to which prayer directs us. 'The chief end of human beings is to glorify God and enjoy him for ever.'[39] We may understand the word 'enjoy' a little differently to the seventeenth-century writers of this Westminster Confession, but it does reflect the joy expressed in Luke's gospel.

I believe that the embrace in Luke 15 is a key picture in the gospel – the kiss of God. No wonder Luke is unwilling to describe the kiss Judas gives to betray Jesus. While Mark and Matthew tell quite clearly that Judas kissed Jesus in the garden of Gethsemane, Luke leaves the actual kiss unspoken: 'Judas approached Jesus to kiss him, but Jesus asked him "Judas are you betraying the Son of Man with a kiss?" ' (22:47). The words are full of pathos – the holy kiss is blasphemed.

There is, however, one other echo of the kiss of God within the gospel. It is in the story of the woman who anoints Jesus in the house of Simon, a story which has plenty of parallels with the anointing stories in the other gospels and yet is placed in a very different setting in Luke's gospel. In Luke's telling of the story, the anointing is taken out of its setting within the events leading up to the passion and ceases to be a preparation for Jesus' burial. Instead it is set in the early part of Jesus' ministry, as people respond to Jesus' words and actions in different ways – some with joy, others with suspicion. Within the story the woman who anoints and kisses Jesus' feet echoes the younger son returning humbled to his father. Simon the Pharisee, who fails to give Jesus a proper welcome, echoes the older son's refusal to share in the father's joy at the return of the lost one. Simon gives Jesus no water to wash his feet, no welcome kiss, no anointing oil. The woman's actions on the other hand show that she is forgiven and loves much; she can go home in peace, knowing the loving embrace of God through Jesus' words and actions.

We in our own context and situation are faced with the same choice to accept the loving embrace of God or to turn our backs on that embrace; to live in the light and power of that loving acceptance or to try to make our own way through life. But still we hesitate, doubting perhaps ourselves (are we deluding ourselves, whistling in the dark, having a fix of the people's opium?) or doubting God (could the Reality that is the source of all reality possibly be interested in our little fumbling lives?). John Betjeman's question in his famous Christmas poem remains our question: 'And is it true? And is it true, this most tremendous tale of all?'[40]

On one level the parable of the loving father is just a story. It is made up. Scholars would disagree as to whether it was a story told by Jesus or by later Christians in the light of Jesus. The witness of Luke – to give us authentic/reliable knowledge – cannot guarantee the truth, however honoured a place his gospel has within Christian tradition. For Luke and his readers truth is not a 'something' that can be arrived at by detached external observation. Truth is a reality that has to be entered into: we have to step into it. That risk of faith is not something we can take on our own; we need the encouragement of a community of faith and above all the encouragement of the Spirit of God, bringing us to our senses and giving us new breath. The story speaks, the picture becomes alive and our hearts burn within us. We are embraced by the silent grace of God.

∞

We have come home, dear Father,
to be held and fed, forgiven and freed
and sent out to draw others to your love, in Christ.
Amen.

A Pattern for Prayer

Introducing a pattern for prayer

I am inviting you to reflect on Luke's gospel over a period of forty days, exploring how forty passages take us deeper into true prayer and intimacy with the One who is here and now reaching out to embrace us.

You may wish to use the following pattern of prayer, which draws from the four gospels, to provide the setting for your reading of Luke. It consists of seven sections but can be used very flexibly. For example you could use the first three sections – and the last – in the morning and then come back to the other prayers in the evening. You could omit the use of the canticles, psalm-like poems from Luke's gospel, or the written prayers, simply following the headings. You may on different occasions want to focus on thanksgiving, confession or intercession. The pattern is simple enough that it – and some of the key verses – can be memorised and so could be used when walking if that is more helpful. While written for individual use, the pattern could also be used with a prayer partner or small group. It is important that you adapt to your own needs, situation and personality, while not avoiding the real challenge that such gospel praying brings.

The constant pressure on us is to go for a quick fix in prayer and to fail to recognise the patience and persistence required to wait on God and to listen. Quietening our minds and stilling our bodies is an important part of preparing to pray – that going into your own room and shutting the door that Jesus describes in the Sermon on the Mount (Matthew 6:6). But prayer is never simply down to us. It is not some anxiety-ridden striving after the Invisible, but a conversation with One who knows our needs and our hearts. In Karl Barth's affirming words, 'Prayer is a grace, an offer of God.'[41] Jesus often confronts the disciples' anxieties and again in the Sermon on the Mount tells his disciples not to try to impress God by long prayers: 'your Father knows your needs before you ask him' (Matthew 6:8). Prayer is a meeting of human boldness – the persistence to continue to speak to God, whatever we may feel – and God's grace – the patient loving kindness of God for us all, come what may.

A pattern for prayer

1 Preparing to pray

Enter God's presence in stillness, remembering Jesus beside you and seeking the help of the Spirit within you. Enter the room of God's presence, shutting the door behind you:

Prayer (may be repeated):

> Emmanuel – God is with us.
>
> (from Matthew 1:23)
>
> *or*   Blessed be the one
>   who comes in the name of the Lord.
>
> (based on Mark 11:45)
>
> *or*   Glory to God in the highest
>   and peace on earth.
>
> (based on Luke 2:14)
>
> *or*   It is the Spirit that gives life.
>
> (from John 6:63)

2 Seeking God's mercy

Reflect on the ways in which you have distanced yourself from God, drawn back from love for God and neighbour:

> Hear, O Israel, the Lord our God, the Lord is one; you shall love the Lord your God with all your heart, and with all your soul and with all your mind and with all your strength. And you shall love your neighbour as yourself.
>
> (Mark 12:29–31)

Prayer (may be repeated):

> Lord, have mercy on me, a sinner.
>
> (based on Luke 18:13)

Assurance: Jesus says: 'Friend, your sins are forgiven.'

> (based on Luke 5:20)

You may wish to use one of Luke's Canticles of praise:

Morning: The Benedictus (Luke 1:68–79)

Evening: The Magnificat (Luke 1:46b–55)

3 Hearing the Gospel

Read the gospel passage and reflection; be opened by the Spirit to God's Word, made known in the story of Jesus:

> The Word became flesh and dwelt among us … full of grace and truth.
>
> (from John 1:14)

4 Giving thanks and praying for others

Enter a time of prayer:

> Father, I thank you .... (*name causes of thanksgiving*)
>
> Father, forgive .... (*name people you need to forgive*)
>
> Father, into your hands I commit .... (*name people and situations in need of God's peace, justice or healing*)

5 Sharing the Abba prayer

Join all Jesus' followers in praying a version of the Lord's Prayer (in words familiar to you or in one of the versions below):

Abba, Father, not what I want, but what you want. Amen.

(Mark 14:36)

or   Father, may your name be hallowed.
       Your kingdom come.
       Give us each day our daily bread
       and forgive us our sins,
       for we forgive all who have done us wrong;
       and do not put us to the test. Amen.

(Luke 11:2–4, REB)

or   Our Father in heaven, hallowed be your name,
       your kingdom come, your will be done
       on earth as it is in heaven.
       Give us this day our daily bread.
       And forgive us our debts,
       as we also have forgiven our debtors.
       And do not bring us to the time of trial,
       but rescue us from the evil one. Amen.

(Matthew 6:9–13)

or   Father, glorify your name. Amen.

(John 12:28a)

You may wish to use another of Luke's canticles:

Canticle: Song of Simeon (Luke 2:29–32)

6 Concluding prayer

Morning: Lord Jesus,
            increase our faith,
            renew our love,
            deepen our joy,
            for the sake of the kingdom.

(based on Luke 17:5)

Evening: Lord Jesus,
                stay with us, we pray, for the day is almost over.
                Send your Spirit to empower our lives
                and to make us true witnesses of your life.

(based on Luke 24:29)

7 *Final reflection*

Reflect on one of the following verses:

Christ came not to be served but to serve and to give his life for me
    and for many.
Thanks be to God.

(based on Mark 10:43)

I was lost but now am found; I was dead but now am alive.
Thanks be to God.

(based on Luke 15:32)

Jesus says: 'I am with you always, to the end of time.'
Thanks be to God.

(from Matthew 28:20)

Jesus says: 'Peace be with you. As the Father has sent me, so I send
    you.'
Thanks be to God.

(from John 20:21)

Move out of praying, recognising the touch and blessing of God on your life.

III

Forty Reflections

The forty reflections and prayers offered in this volume are there to encourage you to pray with Luke's gospel in your own way and situation. Reading the words of the gospel remain of first importance; the reflections and prayers are secondary. Each dwell on a key passage, some just a few verses long, others much longer. Because these do not cover the whole gospel, additional passages are included that will enable you to read the whole of this extraordinary testimony to the way of Jesus.

1 Your prayer has been heard

Read Luke 1:1–17.

> *But the angel said to him, 'Do not be afraid, Zechariah, for your prayer has been heard. Your wife Elizabeth will bear a son and you will name him John.' (Luke 1:13)*

After his very correct and proper introduction, written in 'the delicately balanced style of classical rhetoric'[42] and addressed directly to the reader, Luke turns to the form and style of the Hebrew Scriptures to tell his story. The story he tells begins with an answered prayer: the desperate prayer of an elderly couple who have lived good obedient lives and yet have felt shame and despair over the fact that they have been childless. Their society regards childlessness as a curse from God, a judgement over some hidden failing or wickedness. They go on with their faithful routines; Zechariah has the privilege of being a priest, but the disgrace and grief does not go away.

To have a child is perhaps one of the deepest of all human instincts – often recognised as such only when it proves difficult or impossible to achieve.

Perhaps Zechariah and Elizabeth had accepted their 'fate'; without modern medical knowledge they assumed Elizabeth was 'barren'. Certainly when confronted with an angelic message that Elizabeth will bear him a son Zechariah's reaction is incredulity: are you sure?! After all, he goes on, I'm an old man and my wife is getting on a bit.

An answered prayer: an answer, but of course like all 'answered prayer' it raises as many questions as it answers. The little prayer is to be answered – they will have a son who will be a joy and delight to them.

And this is part of God's answering of a bigger prayer. The desperate cry of an elderly couple is weaved into a greater purpose, God's saving work, God's new dawn for the whole world.

Reflect and pray

Lord God,
  God of Abraham and Sarah
  God of Hannah and Elkanah
  God of Ruth and Boaz
  God of Zechariah and Elizabeth
we thank you for hearing the cries of your people,
the little desperate prayers offered to you
in the darkness of the night.
We thank you for weaving those cries
into your greater purpose of love,
your work of healing and saving,
guiding and renewing.
Hear our little stumbling prayers
and work them into your tapestry of grace and hope.
Uphold us in the waiting times,
the desperate times, the hopeless times.
By your Spirit renew our trust in your greater love,
in Jesus' name.

2 Standing in the presence of God

Read Luke 1:18–25.

> *The angel replied, 'I am Gabriel. I stand in the presence of God, and I have been sent to speak to you and to bring you this good news.'* (*Luke 1:19*)

Gabriel is unused to being questioned. Angels after all are only messengers. They are not mediators or intermediaries, nor there to argue their case, or make some compromise. They are simply deliverers – the message is all important.

But poor old Zechariah cannot take it in. Gabriel stands on his dignity and gives his angelic name. I am Gabriel and I stand in the presence of God and I have been sent to speak to you and to tell you this good news.

Then he tells Zechariah that he will be silent until the day of John's birth, because he did not believe his words. Gabriel, it seems, is allowed to exact minor punishment on those who don't listen. We are not told of Elizabeth's view of the fact that her husband couldn't speak for nine months!

Our questions and doubts are put into perspective when we sense the wonder of God's reality, the glory and majesty of his presence, the greatness of his purposes. Too much of our praying is chatter or tedious repetition and too little is silent waiting and wondering. Christianity is about God's Living Word spoken to us and our world in the story of Jesus, yet all too often it has lost its focus on God's Word of love and become awfully wordy.

Prayer isn't about bombarding God with our wish lists or demands, our successes or failings. Prayer at its truest is waiting on God and discovering the deep silent music of God's grace stirring in our hearts.

Reflect and pray

We stand in your presence, awesome God.
We are silenced,
  our minds cannot grasp your greatness,
  our hearts remain unsure, unknowing,
  our lives untouched, resistant to your Spirit.
We are silenced.
Forgive us
  our faithless fear,
  our timid response,
  our tiresome questions.
Hold us in the silence,
the stillness, the surrendering,
enough to know
that we stand in your presence,
awesome, forgiving God.

3 Yes to God

Read Luke 1:26–38.

> *Then Mary said, 'Here am I, the servant of the Lord; let it be with me*
> *according to your word.' (Luke 1:38)*

Gabriel returns to his work as messenger in the sixth month of Elizabeth's pregnancy. Luke is fascinated by the interaction of the eternal and the temporal – and he roots these early chapters in particular historical political times – the time of Herod the King, the time Caesar Augustus issued a census, the fifteenth year of the reign of Emperor Tiberius. But he has another timescale here – the time of Elizabeth (and then Mary's) pregnancy. Prayer is partly about recognising this interaction of God's time and human time.

Gabriel greets Mary in exalted tones – 'Greetings you who are highly favoured. The Lord is with you' – but Mary is far from reassured. All the religious pictures of Mary receiving Gabriel with calm maiden dignity ignore the reality of the story. Mary is deeply troubled at his words and wonders what kind of greeting this may be. Told that she is to have a child, she asks in shocked tones, 'How will this be?'

She's told that nothing is impossible for God – here surely the questions did not disappear. Rather it was an act of supreme trust – utter faith in God's graciousness – that allowed her to say, 'I am the Lord's servant, let it be …' That 'let it be' echoes God's creative word 'let there be' at the very beginning of creation. The God who brought life out of nothingness has acted again to let there be a new creation.

Reflect and pray

Guard us good Lord
from the easy yes,
the glib promises of faithfulness,
the familiar phrases of religion.
Confront us with your world-turning reality,
your hopes and dreams for our lives.
Help us through the struggles of faith,
that your promises may be known in us
and that we may truly, honestly answer
that we are your servants
seeking your kingdom,
willing your will
to be done in us
and our world.

4 Mary's song: love's laughter

Read Luke 1:39–56.

'My spirit rejoices in God my saviour.' (Luke 1:47)

Without a word about Joseph, Luke follows Mary's great 'let it be' with her hurrying off to Elizabeth's house (again Zechariah the man does not get a look in, apart from owning the house). This is a private female world – the anxious first months of Mary's pregnancy, when the risk of miscarriage is all too possible, and the joyful kicking of the child in Elizabeth's womb, now six months since conception. The male political calendar (the days of King Herod in 1:5 and the time when Quirinius was governor of Syria in 2:2) is forgotten and we enter a deeper and more primitive calendar marked out in the swelling of a mother's womb (1:26, 57; 2:6).

How Luke's male hearers reacted to this glimpse into a private female world is difficult to know, but there is a deep sense of wonder, privilege and subversive joy surrounding Luke's portrayal of the women's time together: the final three months of Elizabeth's pregnancy.

Elizabeth, filled with the Holy Spirit, blesses Mary: 'Blessed are you among women and blessed is the fruit of your womb' (1:42), and tells how at the sound of Mary's greeting the child within her leapt for joy (1:44). Here is the first of many outbursts of joy that will echo repeatedly through Luke's story and it is joy here expressed not by a powerful man or even a faithful woman, but by an unborn child – the ultimate symbol of human vulnerability. The child's kick of joy is taken up by Mary herself as Luke provides her with the first of the great canticles in this overture to the gospel. Again it turns our notions of power and riches upside down.

Reflect on Mary's song and pray

Great, Great God,
laughter swells within me.
Joy and wonder overflow.
You are at work,
even in this –
a child growing like countless others before and since.
You are at work,
to save, to bless, to rescue.
Your love is so tender and so strong,
Holy, Holy God.
You are at work,
glorious and majestic, deep and awesome.
The proud and mighty are shown their places.
The rich and self-satisfied are shown their emptiness.
The poor and hungry are welcomed
and fed not with scraps but with the finest food.
The little people are lifted high.
You are at work,
in the story of Israel,
    Abraham and Sarah and all their offspring,
in the story of this child, Jesus,
    and all who act on his word.
You are at work.

5 A new name and a new dawn

Read Luke 1:57–79.

> By the tender mercy of our God,
>   the dawn from on high will break upon us,
> to give light to those in darkness who sit in darkness and in the shadow
>   of death,
> to guide our feet into the way of peace. (Luke 1:78–79)

The story of the naming of Zechariah and Elizabeth's child has elements that will be repeated again and again in Luke's gospel: the working of God's grace, the debate and confusion leading to a new insight, the sense of wonder and awe ending on a note of joy and praise. It all centres on the child's name and the fact that Elizabeth and Zechariah are breaking with tradition by not naming their firstborn after the father himself. Zechariah has been dumbstruck since meeting with the angel of the Lord in the temple and so is not able to give the child his chosen name. Instead Elizabeth has to stand up to her neighbours and relatives who assume that the child will be named Zechariah (meaning 'the Lord remembers') and certainly not John ('the Lord is gracious'), a name that has no pedigree within the family. A new dawn is coming, new wine is being poured and so this child, who will prepare the way for the new life-giver, is called by a new unfamiliar name.

Zechariah's miraculous confirmation of Elizabeth's determination to call her son John – by writing the name on a tablet – becomes the talk of the neighbourhood, bringing fear, awe and reflection. Zechariah's tongue is loosened and his first words are not a curse on silencing angels but of praise to the glorious God, who has given him the gift of a son and the world the gift of salvation. Behind all the strangeness of the events is the hand – the touch – of a God who brings new hope and life. Luke writes that all who heard of these events pondered them and asked the question, 'What will this child become?' He is signalling even in this early stage that the story requires pondering by all who hear it – it requires a deep listening from the heart.

Filled with the Holy Spirit, Zechariah gives his prophetic song. In one sense it should be about John, the child who is the prophet of the Most High, going before the Lord to prepare his way. Yet, in fact, apart from the one verse that speaks of 'you child' (1:76) the focus is on God and the new dawn that God will bring in fulfilment of the promises made long ago. The new dawn is coming as God remembers the holy covenant and brings salvation and forgiveness, light and peace, through Jesus.

This great song of the new dawn is rooted not simply in the story of Zechariah and his child John, but in the event of Jesus, the worship of Luke's Christian community and the worship of the Church since that day. As we use it within our own worship today – personally and corporately – we join with the whole community of faith in praising the God who looks upon us and this world so graciously and tenderly. We affirm with all God's people that the dawn has come and will come.

Reflect and pray

Jesus, in your conception through the Spirit's power
    and Mary's humble obedience,
  the dawn has come, **to bring us light and peace.**
In your birth in poverty, with nothing but love,
  the dawn has come, **to bring us light and peace.**
In your childhood with its hidden-ness,
    growth and grace,
  the dawn has come, **to bring us light and peace.**
In your baptism, opening heaven itself
    with the Lover's joy in the beloved,
  the dawn has come, **to bring us light and peace.**
In your struggle with the evil one
    and your rejection of the easy way,
  the dawn has come, **to bring us light and peace.**

In your proclamation of good news to the poor
    and release to the captives,
  the dawn has come, **to bring us light and peace.**
In your calling of the disciples to follow you
    and not to be afraid,
  the dawn has come, **to bring us light and peace.**
In your healing of the sick and compassion
    for the outcaste,
  the dawn has come, **to bring us light and peace.**
In your love for your enemies and prayers
    for the wicked,
  the dawn has come, **to bring us light and peace.**
In your acceptance of a woman's kiss and tears
    and the forgiveness you gave,
  the dawn has come, **to bring us light and peace.**
In your prayer through the night and your dazzling
    brightness on the mountaintop,
  the dawn has come, **to bring us light and peace.**
In your weeping over Jerusalem
    and entry as king of peace,
  the dawn has come, **to bring us light and peace.**
In your prayer that God's will might be done
    and your arrest for our sake,
  the dawn has come, **to bring us light and peace.**
In your look of compassion at Peter
    who denied knowing you,
  the dawn has come, **to bring us light and peace.**
In your naked love upon a cross,
  the dawn has come, **to bring us light and peace.**
In your death, when the sun's light failed,
  the dawn has come, **to bring us light and peace.**
In your burial in the rock-hewn tomb,
    witnessed by the women,
  the dawn has come, **to bring us light and peace.**
In your resting on the Sabbath
    in the mystery of death,
  the dawn has come, **to bring us light and peace.**

In your glorious rising again, as Living Lord,
   the dawn has come, **to bring us light and peace.**
In your walking with the disciples on the road,
      making their hearts burn within them,
   the dawn has come, **to bring us light and peace.**
In your breaking of bread to open their eyes
      to your presence,
   the dawn has come, **to bring us light and peace.**
In your promise of the Spirit's liberating power,
   the dawn has come, **to bring us light and peace.**
In your blessing from heaven,
      bringing great joy and worship,
   the dawn has come, **to bring us light and peace.**
Blessed be your name, Lord Jesus Christ,
now and for ever.

6 No room

Read Luke 2:1–7.

She gave birth to her firstborn and wrapped him in bands of cloth, and laid him in a manger because there was no room for them in the inn. (Luke 2:7)

Luke relates Jesus' birth to the worldwide census (worldwide in Roman terms at least) to hint at its worldwide significance. He associates Jesus' birth with the reign of the famous Emperor Augustus – an emperor linked to an era of Roman peace, *Pax Augusta* – to suggest that the real bearer of peace and salvation is a child placed in a manger in the insignificant town of Bethlehem.

He intertwines Roman and Jewish history bringing together within the story the names of Augustus and Quirinius on the one hand and Judaea, David and Bethlehem on the other. The child is thus shown to be significant to both Jewish and Gentile worlds.

The story of the birth itself has Old Testament allusions, which would echo in the minds of the gospel-hearers. The manger might well have been regarded as a sign of God's sustenance of his people, reminding hearers of the Septuagint version of Isaiah 1:3: 'An ox knows its owner and an ass the manger of its Lord; but Israel knows not me, and my people do not comprehend.'[43] So Jesus is born in obscurity – excluded – but at the same time is the true sustainer and saviour of his people, Jew and Gentile alike.

It is clear that for Luke 'the child lying in a manger' is a crucial and powerful sign of the kind of Messiah Jesus is to be. Within this second chapter he uses the phrase three times: first, Mary lays Jesus 'in a manger, because there was no room in the inn' (2:7); then the angel of the Lord announces to the shepherds that confirmation of his joyful message of a Saviour born this day will be this: 'you will find a child wrapped in bands of cloth and lying in a manger'

(2:12); finally, the shepherds go to Bethlehem and find 'Mary and Joseph and the child lying in manger' (2:16). Luke sets up a very deliberate contrast within the story between the power of the Emperor Augustus and the vulnerable child, the power of state and the glory of God: here is a Saviour and Messiah who will turn the world upside down.

The challenge to the modern reader, who may be so familiar with this story from carol services, is to hear again Luke's subtle interweaving of political and divine history, to see the vulnerable hungry child as the true source of nourishment for the deepest hunger of humanity, and to make room for his time-shattering reality here and now.

Reflect on the child placed in the manger

Census

    Taxes

        Forms

            Politics

                Government

                    Registers

                    Travel

                      Family

                        History

                            Promises

                            Hopes

                            Fears

                        Crowds

                    Commerce

                  Business

            Noise

          Pressure

      Time

     Grace

   A child

  A manger

No room?

7 Glory to God

Read Luke 2:8–20.

> *Glory to God in the highest heaven,*
> *and on earth peace among those whom he favours.* (*Luke 2:14*)

Typically of Luke it is people on the margins of society who are the first to hear the glorious news of the birth of the child, born as Saviour and Messiah, yet born in poverty and obscurity, lying in a manger in Bethlehem. The shepherds are virtual outcastes of their own society, ritually unclean and with a dubious reputation, despite the great King David having once been himself a shepherd. They watch their flock just as the great God watches over his great flock of humanity. The angel's news brings the shepherds, first, fear, then curiosity, then joy and praise for God. As they return from having seen the child in the manger they echo the song of the angels, 'glorifying and praising God for all they had heard and seen'. This echo of earthly and heavenly joy will be repeated many times in the gospel and is stressed in the great stories of the lost being found. Once more the joy of a shepherd (over a lost sheep found) will echo the angel's joy (over those who turn back to God).

Luke turns up the volume at this point in the story, underlining the incredible importance of this child who is placed in the manger. The whole heavenly host are wheeled out to emphasise that God is at work and a new dawn has come on earth. The twin themes of the angels' song – 'Glory to God' and 'peace on earth' – are the essence of the Gospel that will be lived out in the child born as Saviour, Messiah and Lord.

Reflect and pray

With the angels and shepherds we give our praise:
Glory to you our God, Lord of heaven and earth.
We have heard your voice, in the story of the child
born in poverty, bringing delight to Mary and
Joseph, joy to the shepherds and the ordinary
people, hope to the world:
With the angels and shepherds we give our praise:
Glory to you our God, Lord of heaven and earth.
We have seen your presence in Jesus, the servant
Lord, so close to your heart, opening your grace,
your forgiveness, your life to us:
With the angels and shepherds we give our praise:
Glory to you our God, Lord of heaven and earth.
We have felt your touch in these treasures of faith,
these saving stories from the past, these powerful
pointers to your Spirit's work here and now, these
sure signs of hope for the future:
With the angels and shepherds we give our praise:
Glory to you our God, Lord of heaven and earth.
We have received your challenge to seek your
presence in the ordinary places of life, to accept your
shocking grace, and to share your good news with a
needy world:
With the angels and shepherds we give our praise:
Glory to you our God, Lord of heaven and earth.
We have glimpsed your vision for the world, of
conflict ended, justice restored, relationships mended
and fear destroyed and we will walk your way of
peace:
With the angels and shepherds we give our praise:
Glory to you our God, Lord of heaven and earth.

8 Seeing salvation

Read Luke 2:21–40.

'For my own eyes have seen the salvation, which you have prepared in the presence of all people.' (Luke 2:30–31)

The angels have returned to heaven and the shepherds to the fields. Now Mary and Joseph undertake to strictly fulfil the requirements of the Jewish law and tradition. Their child is circumcised on the eighth day, named Jesus and then, after the full forty-day period of Mary's purification, presented at the Jerusalem temple. Luke seems to delight at this point in explaining the traditional rites of the Jewish law, reminding his Gentile readers that according to the law 'every firstborn male shall be designated as holy to the Lord' (2:22). The fact that he seems to conflate the two ceremonies of redeeming the firstborn and purification of the mother may betray his Gentile background, but is not in itself significant.

Within this story of traditional Jewish piety, the reader is given another glimpse of the essence of who this child is. Simeon and Anna speak about the child who is to bring salvation, light to the Gentiles and glory to Israel, a sign that will be accepted by some and rejected by others. Luke's linking of a man and a woman, a priest and a prophet is intentional and characteristic, as he tells this all-inclusive story which points toward the cross.

Simeon's words – the canticle known today as the Nunc Dimittis – speak of the child being the bringer of peace, salvation and light not simply to his own nation but for all peoples.

Reflect on how Simeon saw salvation and how we see it today

Here is the peace of God,
the Word of grace and truth made flesh and blood
and held in an old man's arms.

Here is the light to the Gentiles,
not in the power of empire
or the wealth of nations
but in a screaming child,
held in an old man's arms.

Here is the glory of Israel
not in a nation conquering the world in God's name
or a land purified of all foreign presence,
but in a quietened child,
held in an old man's arms.

It is enough to see that child
to feel the touch of his fingers,
the warmth of his body,
the breeze of his breath.
It is enough to sense the hope
and the pain, the piercing challenge
and the glorious blessing.
It is enough
to know the difficult peace
this child brings to this broken world,

Glory to God, in the name of Jesus,
Saviour, Light and Peace.

(Further passage: Luke 2:41–52. Reflect on Jesus' presence in his Father's house and the reaction of Mary and Joseph.)

9 Heaven breaks open

Read Luke 3:21–22 (3:1–38).

> *… when Jesus also had been baptised and was praying, the heaven was opened … (Luke 3:21)*

This is such a critical early moment in the gospel. Luke retells Mark's account in an immensely careful and powerful way. The focus is wholly on Jesus, with John removed from the picture in the previous passage (with a note about John being shut up in prison in 3:20) and no mention made of John baptising Jesus. Instead Luke simply describes the baptism as having taken place: '… and when Jesus had also been baptised …' (3:21). He places his emphasis on Jesus' praying rather than on the action of John or the water of the Jordan. It is as Jesus is praying that things happen; the Holy Spirit descends like a dove and a voice comes from heaven. The two crucial themes that will echo down the gospel are expressed in one simple verse: the themes of the action of the Holy Spirit and God's Word of love.

For Luke the Spirit's filling of Jesus is no vague or nebulous emotional or psychological experience. He emphasises the reality of the event by speaking of the Holy Spirit as descending on Jesus 'in bodily form like a dove'. Scholars argue over what the symbolism of the dove means, pointing to possible echoes of the Spirit sweeping over the waters in creation (Genesis 1:2), or the dove released by Noah (Genesis 8:8), both of which speak of new creation or deliverance. Luke will give other symbols of the Holy Spirit in Acts in describing the work of the Spirit as like a strong wind and tongues of fire. The picture of the dove is found in all the gospels in their description of the Spirit's descent on Jesus at his baptism and was clearly a widely accepted picture of the Spirit's touch among the early Christians. Perhaps it can speak to us of the Spirit's freedom like a bird of peace, sacrifice and hope.

The Spirit descends and a voice comes from heaven. Only in one other point in Luke's narrative is God's voice heard: the equally critical moment on the mountain at the transfiguration as Jesus prepares for the next stage of his ministry, the journey to Jerusalem (9:35). Later in a speech to the Gentiles Peter reflects that after the baptism John announced, 'God anointed Jesus of Nazareth with the Holy Spirit and power' (Acts 10:18). God's loving affirmation of Jesus in the key moments of baptism and transfiguration contrasts to the only other point in the gospel when God speaks, addressing the rich barn-builder in Jesus' parable as 'You fool …' (12:20). It is obvious who in Luke's eyes is 'rich towards God' (12:21) and of course the good news is that the love expressed by God towards the beloved is open to us too.

Reflect and pray

Heaven breaks open,
   for you, Lord Jesus, enter the depths of human life.
Heaven breaks open,
   for you, Lord Jesus, pray from the centre
     of your soul.
Heaven breaks open,
   for you, Lord Jesus, receive the Spirit's
     gentle power.
Heaven breaks open,
   for you, Lord Jesus, know the wonder
     of God's love and blessing.
Heaven breaks open,
   for you, Lord Jesus, bring joy and delight
     to the one who sent you.
Heaven breaks open,
   for you, Lord Jesus, call us to share your life today:
   to reach out to everyday people,
   to pray from the centre of our souls,
   to receive your Spirit,
   to know the wonder of God's love
   and so to bring joy in heaven, peace on earth
     and glory to God's name.

Heaven breaks open.

Lord Jesus, break open our hearts and minds,
    by the Spirit's flight,
and raise us up to live your way.

10 Testing to the limit

Read Luke 4:1-13.

Jesus, full of the Holy Spirit, was led by the Spirit into the wilderness.
(*Luke 4:1*)

A key element of prayer in Luke's gospel is about holding on to the Word of God, allowing that Word spoken in the Hebrew Scriptures and proclaimed in the Christian Gospel to guide and uphold and bear fruit in our lives. Other recurring themes are the need to persevere and not to give up and our need of the Spirit's help. All three of these elements are present in Luke's account of Jesus' time of testing in the wilderness.

This comes at a crucial moment in Jesus' life, as he begins his public ministry. His baptism has been a moment of affirmation and anointing; as he prays, the Holy Spirit descends on him and a voice from heaven addresses him: 'You are my son, the beloved, with you I am well pleased.' In the power of that Spirit, Jesus will soon be travelling around Galilee, proclaiming God's kingdom and the good news of liberation and hope. But first the Spirit leads him into the wilderness to wrestle with the reality and nature of that sonship and mission.

The three temptations echo the three key challenges to Jesus and centre on his relationship to God. The struggle within Jesus is portrayed – by Jesus himself and by the gospel-writers – as a vivid encounter between supreme good and supreme evil, between Jesus and the devil. Each time the devil spits out the words 'If you are the son of God …', challenging Jesus to use this relationship in a way that would twist his mission and destroy that union with God. Each time Jesus shouts back his defence with words from the book of Deuteronomy, part of the holy Torah which describes the fundamentals of the relationship between God and his people Israel.

Here is a picture of prayer as wrestling, and in Luke's account wrestling without the comfort of angels. This wrestling ends with the chilling words, 'the devil departed from Jesus until an opportune time'. Luke is clear that the great test, the final temptation for Jesus – in Jerusalem – is yet to come.

Reflect and pray

Uncomfortable God,
guard us from treating you as a soft blanket,
   a reassuring stick,
   a puppet of our own making;
pour out your untamed Spirit
   into our hearts and minds and bodies
to fill us with your life,
to lead us out into the wilderness,
to silence our inner chatter,
to confront us with what is real – good and evil.

Uncomfortable God,
guard us from temptation;
forgive us when we feed our bodies
   and forget our souls;
forgive us when we look to our own glory
   and fail to worship you;
forgive us when we test you
   rather than trust your faithful presence.

Uncomfortable God,
turn us to Christ, the disturbing Saviour,
who faced the full force of temptation
and the evil one himself in the silence of the desert
and held on to you, the Lord, the God of all.

11 God's today

Read Luke 4:14–44.

And he began to say to them: 'Today this scripture has been fulfilled in your hearing.' (Luke 4:21)

Written words always come from the past, yet they can on occasion take on new life and present power. This is what happens as Jesus reads a passage of Scripture in the synagogue in his home town of Nazareth. The words of Isaiah cease to be words from an ancient past, but become words addressed directly to every one of his hearers, words coming true as they hear them. Jesus' solemn announcement that 'Today, this scripture has been fulfilled' effectively enacts those words – if his hearers are willing to absorb them. He will use the same 'today' (*semeron*) in announcing that salvation has come to the house of Zacchaeus (19:9) and that the penitent thief will be with him in paradise (23:43). This 'today' is not simply a matter of powerful oratory, it is a breaking in of God's now.

Walter Brueggemann writes of those occasions when the Spirit speaks anew through the words of Scripture, almost in spite of the limitations we bring to it, to lead us in what is 'strange and new': 'The script of the book is a host and launching pad for the wind among us that the world cannot evoke and the church cannot resist.'[44]

Isaiah becomes the launching pad for Jesus' mission to his people and beyond.

The initial reaction to Jesus' announcement is positive, as people sense the moment, but then nagging questions start to rumble around the congregation. They find it impossible to relate what they are hearing and experiencing – the now of God's Word – with their prejudices and preconceptions about who Jesus is – the son of Joseph, the carpenter. As Jesus picks up the uncertainty

of his hearers he moves into deeper controversy by interpreting
Scripture in a way that confronts other prejudices and preconceptions. The crowd responds angrily and violently, but Jesus walks
on, following the way that will lead to a cross. Jesus is always on the
move, pausing only to slip into the hills to seek the Father's will
and rest in God's presence (4:42).

Reflect and pray

I will celebrate this day
the God who speaks and speaks
and speaks again.

I will give thanks for the prophets of the past,
the Isaiahs of ancient times
whose words still burn in hearts today,
words of liberation for the oppressed,
good news for the poor,
freedom for captives,
sight for all blinded by fear.

I will give thanks for the carpenter's son,
who took old words and made them present,
living them in all he said and did,
breaking the confines of sacred space,
opening life to those long despised and rejected,
disturbing hardened minds and stifled hearts.

I will give thanks for the friend of God's friend,
gathering those words for his own moment of now,
his own people with all they faced,
making the words of Jesus live again.

And I will give thanks for these words
read and spoken again
in my time, my place, my world.

Miracle of miracles,
the Word lives again,
  liberating
  disturbing
  opening up life
the word of Isaiah,
the word of Jesus,
the word of Luke,
the Living Word of the Living God
who speaks and speaks
and speaks again.

12 Caught in God's net

Read Luke chapters 5 and 6.

> *'Why do you call me "Lord, Lord" and do not do what I tell you?'*
> *(Luke 6:46)*

Beginning with the call of Simon Peter and then Levi, these chapters take us onwards to the choosing of the twelve apostles, for which Jesus prepares by praying to God through the night (6:12). Peter's cry, 'Go away from me, Lord, for I am a sinful man', is followed by the cry of the leper, 'Lord, if you choose, you can make me clean.' Yet for both Jesus does not fear the contamination either of sin or illness, stretching out to both in reassurance and grace. He tells Simon that he too will be caught up in the stretching-out work, this catching people in the embrace of God.

Jesus' healing and teaching ministry are intertwined within these chapters culminating in 'the sermon on the plain', a collection of sayings which has parallels to Matthew's Sermon on the Mount. The table-turning nature of the gospel is once again expressed through the series of blessings for the poor, hungry and sorrowful and woes for the rich, full and self-satisfied. Love is to be both stretched (even to include enemies) and to be deepened (to reflect God's compassion and forgiveness). The chapters close with stark choices between bearing good and bad fruit, being built on rock or sand, with Jesus inviting all: 'Come to me, hear my words and act on them.'

Reflect and pray

Lord Jesus, your words burn in our minds and souls
and like Peter we are afraid,
fearful of the change you will bring to our lives

this and every day.
Speak your word of grace to us once more,
calling us so powerfully to banish our fears,
to come to you, to hear your word,
to act on all you say.

Lord, have mercy and make us merciful.
Lord, show forgiveness and help us to forgive.
Lord, reveal your kindness and make us kinder.
Stretch our love by your love.
Stretch it to those we so easily judge and condemn.
Stretch it to those we loathe or fear.
Stretch it to those we pass by or ignore.

By your Spirit turn us into better trees;
transform our thorns and brambles
   into fruiting branches
and make our hearts abundant, generous and useful,
good soil in which your kingdom seed may grow
and bear good fruit for our wounded world.

13 Only speak the word, Lord

Read Luke 7:1–10.

A centurion there had a slave whom he valued highly and who was ill and close to death. (Luke 7:2)

Luke brings together a series of encounters between Jesus and people of varied backgrounds. His choice balances the responses of men and women, Gentiles and Jews, rich and poor. So the story of a Gentile centurion in Capernaum is followed by a widow from Nain, mention of Jesus' reputation throughout Judaea and the surrounding country, the response of John the Baptist and his disciples, and then the woman anointing Jesus' feet and the many women who supported his ministry. Luke carefully arranges his material to show the favourable response of ordinary people to Jesus: '[The crowd] glorified God, saying, "A great prophet has risen among us!" and "God has looked favourably on his people" ' (7:16).

What this series of stories expresses is a recognition of the authority of Jesus – his power to heal and save, to bring good news and blessing to people's lives. The series begins with the story of a centurion whose servant is desperately ill. Both Matthew and Luke have learnt this story from a common source, but both tell it in their own particular way. While Matthew describes a direct conversation between the centurion and Jesus, Luke seems determined to keep the centurion at a distance, with first a delegation of town elders making the request on his behalf and then a group of friends reporting his words to Jesus.

It is as if Luke is emphasising that one does not need to meet Jesus 'in the flesh' to put one's faith in him and recognise his authority as healer and saviour. The centurion is described in four ways in the story:

1   Luke introduces the man simply as a centurion who has a
     slave whom he highly values and who is dangerously ill.
     The attention is placed on the servant – as one who is
     valued and in danger.
2   The Jewish elders describe the man as worthy of Jesus'
     attention, one who loves the Jewish people (and is by
     implication a 'God fearer') and built the local synagogue.
3   The centurion – through his friends – describes himself as
     not worthy to have Jesus come under his roof, but also as
     one who recognises what authority is about.
4   Jesus describes the man, with amazement, as one of
     unparalleled faith.

Jesus' words are the climax to the story; the challenge to his hearers
(and the gospel readers) is to respond with similar intensity and
compassion. The centurion's faith is totally focused away from
himself towards Jesus and towards the need of his servant. The final
line of the story is almost an afterthought: the servant is found in
good health when the friends return to the house. Luke's focus has
been on the nature of faith: the specifics of the story – with its very
different culture (one of an occupying military force, slavery and
the complex first-century relationships of Jews and Gentiles) and
the mystery of the healing itself – are secondary to the call to a faith
that is self-forgetting and focused on the compassionate authority
of Jesus.

Reflect and pray

Authority frightens us.
Our minds tainted
with all we see of power's corruption,
words used so easily,
promises made so lightly.
When it comes to the moment of decision,
that step of utter foolish faith,
we hold back.
We hold on to our need to control the outcome,
to be sure that we will not be fooled.

Jesus, remind us of the centurion,
who amazed you with his faith,
who refused to trouble you,
refused to receive you in his home,
refused to meet you face to face,
yet recognised in you one under divine authority
and made that step of total trust:
'Only speak the word, Lord,
and let my servant be healed.'

True and gracious Lord,
by your liberating Word
enable us to let go of our pride,
our fear, our distrust,
that we ourselves may be healed,
made whole by your command.

(Further passage: Luke 7:11–35. Reflect on Jesus' words of comfort, challenge and wisdom.)

14 A woman's love for Jesus

Read Luke 7:36–50.

'... hence she has shown great love ...' (*Luke 7:47*)

The story of a woman anointing Jesus is contained within each of the gospels, yet in this instance Luke strays quite considerably from Mark's account. In fact he may well have drawn from a different tradition to contrast an unnamed woman with Simon the Pharisee. There is much debate among commentators about Luke's account. Luke tells us very little about the woman apart from that she lived in the city and was a sinner. What was her sin? The assumption down the centuries has been that her sin was sexual by nature, her loose hair assumed to reflect her loose morality as a prostitute. However, more recent feminist commentators have asked if this is a matter of male assumptions distorting the story. After all, Peter calls himself a sinner at his first encounter with Jesus (5:8) and we do not tend to assume his sin was sexual in nature. Are we as guilty as Simon the Pharisee of labelling the woman? Are our Bibles right to entitle the story 'a sinful woman forgiven' or would a better title be 'the woman who loved much'. Reflecting on feminist comments on the passage, Amy-Jill Levine notes: 'the Lukan Jesus seen as praising a woman who is profoundly physical and emotional without shame or hindrance and depicted as enjoying her touch emerges as quite a different Jesus than the one who sponsors a programme of asceticism.'[45] Read the story without the glaze of church propriety and it is an incredibly sensuous, even scandalous, account.

Of course there is much we do not know about the woman quite apart from her name or the nature of her sinning. We only know that she – a sinner – has come to faith, has experienced forgiveness and now in response to that reality comes to anoint

Jesus as an expression of love and thankfulness. When Jesus tells her that her sins are forgiven, he is stating a reality that already exists – shown by her outpouring of love. Jesus explains this very carefully to Simon in his story of the two debtors. The unnamed woman's actions of anointing Jesus do not bring about her forgiveness, but are a response to them. In other words as we read the story of the woman and Jesus, we are called not to judge the woman, but to seek to identify ourselves with her in her utter reckless love for Jesus.

Imagine the woman's prayer

Foolish Lord,
who came to be hung on a tree
   and gave me new life and freedom,
accept my love poured out at your feet,
accept the fragrance of my gifts,
   money spent extravagantly for you,
accept my tears, streaming wantonly,
   wetting your toes,
accept my hair as a towel to dry your skin,
accept my kisses, not face to face,
   but from the dusty ground of my being.

Foolish Lord,
close your ears to the murmuring voices around me
   telling you that I am dirt, a slut, a non-person,
that kind of woman who should be thrown back
   into the gutter;
close your eyes to looks of anger
   and embarrassment,
close your heart to the hurt
   they intend to inflict on you.

Foolish Lord,
thank you for your joy in my tears
   and the washing of your feet,
your joy in my constant kisses and perfumed oil;

thank you for revealing the love within me
and the forgiveness I have received.

Foolish Lord,
send me out in faith, saved by you,
   to live your peace
and help me to know the cost you bear,
the body broken, the blood outpoured,
love stretched to the limit, yet victorious.

(Further passage: Luke 8:1—9:17. Reflect on Jesus' teaching, healing and feeding.)

15 Mountain prayer

Read Luke 9:18–36.

Jesus took with him Peter and John and James, and went up on the mountain to pray. (Luke 9:28)

The story of the transfiguration of Jesus forms a vital staging post in the gospel, following on from Peter's declaration that Jesus is the Messiah and Jesus' announcement of his journey to Jerusalem and rejection there. Luke links them with the phrase 'Now about eight days after these sayings', altering Mark's 'six days later', perhaps to hint that this is a glimpse of the new dawn, the resurrection to come. Characteristically Luke sets the event within the context of Jesus praying, just as he places Jesus' earlier question 'Who do you say I am?' in the same context of prayer.

Here as they watch, the three privileged disciples – Peter, John and James – are shown the necessity of Jesus' exodus or departure, his passion and triumph in Jerusalem, and they glimpse his glory, the glory of which Jesus will speak again after his resurrection (24:26).

The event echoes the earlier moment of divine revelation at the baptism of Jesus as he faced the beginning of his ministry, the only other occasion when the voice from heaven is heard. This time the mysterious voice from the cloud is directed not to Jesus as at the baptism, but to the three disciples: 'This is my Son, my Chosen; listen to him!' (9:35).

The three have seen the glory of Jesus, as he is caught up in the divine presence through prayer, as he is seen in the context of the great lawgiver and prophet who had gone before him, as he sets his face to Jerusalem and his exodus and mission. Though sleepy they have stayed awake – alert to the divine action – and so have been given this vision. But vision is not sufficient: they are now addressed by the divine Reality and told to listen to Jesus. Vision leads on to discernment and obedience – hearing and action. As Jesus has taught earlier, to be Jesus' brothers and sisters – God's sons and daughters – requires them and us 'to hear the word of God and do it' (8:21). That hearing requires alertness, and when they reach Jerusalem, place of Jesus' exodus, Jesus will tell them again of the need to be on their guard and to be alert at all times (21:34–36).

Reflect and pray

Holy Spirit, fire of God,
alongside us and within us,
take us further – further up and further in –
as we pray with Jesus, who prays for us.

Take us further
as we gaze on his face, bright with love,
and are changed by his light shining upon us.

Take us further
as we open the Scriptures and hear
its word of liberation and its call upon our lives.

Take us further
as we take up our cross day by day
and journey with Christ the exodus
which frees us from fear and oppression,
from sin and death.

Holy Spirit, breath of God,
take us further
as you rouse us from our heavy sleep
and open our eyes to the glory of Jesus.

Take us further
as the mystery of God – the cloud of terror and joy –
overshadows, overwhelms and overpowers us.

Take us further
as God speaks the Word of life
and we are led to listen to the beloved.

Take us further
as the vision fades and disappears
and Jesus stands with us alone, now and always.

Take us further
  as we carry the wonder of grace
and the challenge of truth
  into the ordinary world of work and money,
home and family,
time and travel,
politics and lifestyle, laughter and tears.

(Further passage: Luke 9:7–62. Reflect on what happens when Jesus comes down from the mountain and how he then 'set his face to go to Jerusalem'.)

16 The peace mission

Read Luke 10:1–16.

'Whatever house you enter, first say, "Peace to this house!" ' (Luke 10:5)

The sending out of the twelve (9:1–6) is a precursor of this greater mission – the sending out of the seventy – which is itself a foretaste of the greater mission of Acts, where the kingdom news will be proclaimed to all nations beginning in Jerusalem, once the disciples have been clothed with the Holy Spirit.

Here in this mission the Holy Spirit is not referred to directly, but the disciples are sent ahead of Jesus, to prepare his way and are told to pray to 'the Lord of the harvest'. The enlarged group of seventy (or seventy-two – manuscripts vary, but there is no need to quibble over the exact number!) is still seen as wholly inadequate in relation to the harvest that is ready to be gathered. The kingdom message is not for a few, but for all: the Lord desires the healing and rescue of all his children. The fact that some – even many – reject that offer of healing and that word of peace is seen by Luke (and by Jesus himself) as unbearably tragic. The message of peace is paradoxically a cause for conflict and division: 'the falling and rising of many in Israel … a sign that will be opposed' (2:33). Yet despite the opposition the harvest is great and the task of vital importance; the urgent note remains uppermost – the harvest needs desperately to be gathered or it will be spoilt.

The gathering is by word and deed; the two go hand in hand. There is no division between the message of the kingdom and the signs of the kingdom, the word of peace and the work of healing; the spoken and enacted reality that God's kingdom is near go hand in hand.

For those sent out the key elements are peace, simplicity and purity. In an almost tangible way they are to be bearers of God's

peace – God's favour – and are not to be distracted from their task
of bringing this reality to the communities ahead of them. Where
they receive a welcome they are called to stay, to share more fully
that peace-bringing reality with the people; where they are
rejected they are to ritually clean the dust from their feet and move
on.

Reflect on where Jesus is calling you to share his peace

Send us out, Lord,
into our streets and neighbourhoods,
into our villages and towns,
our cities and nations,
our world with all its deep beauty and brutal pain.
Send us out, Lord,
into homes full of emptiness
and lives in need of your fullness.

Keep it simple, Lord.
Take from us
the burdens of status and pride,
position and possessions,
anxiety and fear.
Keep us true to you
and true to your way.

Fill us with your peace, Lord,
that grace and peace may flow;
flow through us to all we meet;
flow through talk at table
and words along the way;
flow through deeds of kindness
and messages of hope.
Fill us with your peace,
to bring healing to your world
and the nearness of your kingdom.

Stay with us, Lord,
that we may stay with others

in all that life brings:
the joy and the hardship,
the love and the hurt,
patiently, persistently sharing your life.
Stay with us, Lord.

Shake from us, Lord,
the dust of cynicism and despair,
the dust of evil and hatred,
the dust of ignorance and folly.
Shake from us
the dust of self-sufficiency and human pride,
the dust that clogs hearts and minds
   and deadens life.

Turn us back, Lord,
to your joy, your peace, your word of life,
that we may ever walk in the light of your dawn.

17 Jesus rejoices

Read Luke 10:17–24.

At that same hour Jesus rejoiced in the Holy Spirit and said, 'I thank you, Father, Lord of heaven and earth …' (Luke 10:21)

Unlike the other gospels, Luke describes two great missions undertaken by the followers of Jesus among the villages of Galilee – first by the twelve and then by the seventy (or seventy-two). The return of the twelve from their mission leads to Jesus withdrawing with them to a private space and then on to the feeding of the five thousand (9:10–17). The return of the seventy, triumphant and joyful, leads to Jesus offering a great prayer of thanksgiving (10:21–22).

This prayer, similar to one in Matthew's gospel (Matthew 11:25–27), is 'a meteorite fallen from the Johannine sky'.[46] Its language and style is much more that of John's gospel than that normally found in the synoptic gospels, evidence of the influence of the Johannine tradition, some years before that gospel was brought to completion.

In recording this prayer, Matthew and Luke share a common source of material, but Luke introduces Jesus' praying with a characteristic emphasis on the Holy Spirit: 'At that same hour Jesus rejoiced in the Holy Spirit and said, "I thank you, Father, Lord of heaven and earth …" ' (10:21).

Here is no precise doctrine of the Trinity; instead we are given a flavour of the divine relationship – Jesus caught up in joy and thanksgiving, under the inspiration of the Holy Spirit, focusing heart and mind on Abba, Father, and aligning himself to the Father's gracious will.

This picture of prayer explodes our attempts to reduce prayer to a technique or a way to 'control' God. Instead it challenges and calls us to align ourselves with Jesus and to come to God as infants, recognising the Father as 'Lord of heaven and earth', and ourselves as dependent on God's grace and Spirit. Humbly and happily we are entering the loving unity of God – parent/child/spirit. Rejoicing in God's Spirit and thanking God for his gracious self-revelation in Christ thus frees us from our self-centred and self-defined praying.

Reflect and use this call to worship

Rejoice, rejoice!
Our names are in heaven's light!
Our souls are kept in the Spirit's care!
Our lives are called to the work of Christ!

Rejoice, rejoice!
God's love cannot be grasped by human minds!
God's life cannot be trapped in human wisdom!
God's Spirit blows as it wills, gracious and free!

Rejoice, rejoice,
in Jesus Christ who shows us the Father's heart,
in Jesus Christ who declares us to be God's children,
in Jesus Christ who calls us to follow his way!

Rejoice, rejoice,
in the Father's faithfulness,
in Jesus' joy,
in the Spirit's surprises,
grace upon grace!

Rejoice, rejoice!
Give thanks this day and each day,
for God's will is so gracious
and God's wisdom is so deep,
through Jesus Christ, the bringer of joy.

18 Christ in the dust

Read Luke 10:25–37.

'A man was going down from Jerusalem …' (Luke 10:30)

Roadways are immensely important in Luke's account. No doubt this in part reflected the reality of the Roman Empire and its vital lines of communication, but for Luke the road can also be a key place of encounter. The road between Jerusalem and Nazareth is the place where Joseph and Mary recognise that the boy Jesus is missing. The road to Jerusalem is one Jesus has to tread on his way to his 'exodus' (9:51) and along that road he meets people who reject and accept him, culminating in the great entrance into Jerusalem. The road between Jerusalem and Emmaus is the place where Cleopas and his companion encounter their risen Lord, who walks alongside them as a stranger and causes their hearts to burn within them. On the road between Jerusalem and Gaza, Philip meets the Ethiopian eunuch and shares his faith in the slaughtered lamb (Acts 8:26). On the road from Jerusalem to Damascus, Saul meets the one whom he is persecuting and starts life anew; a story so important to Luke that it is told three times (Acts 9:1–19; 22:6 –16; 26:12–18).

Roads are significant places of encounter and this is echoed in the great parable of the Good Samaritan, which is set on the road between Jerusalem and Jericho, a dangerous stretch of road, notorious for bandits and muggings. The tensions between Jews and their neighbours the Samaritans have already been underlined in the previous chapter. Jesus has begun his journey to Jerusalem and makes for a Samaritan village on the way, but the villagers turn him and his disciples away. For James and John this is typical behaviour from the half-caste heretics the Samaritans, and in typical hellfire fashion they ask Jesus, 'Lord, do you want us to

command fire to come down from heaven and consume them?'
(9:54). Jesus' response is to rebuke them and simply head for
another village.

There is no doubt that the parable is about recognising the
divine imperative in the needs of our fellow human beings whatever their background. The professional clergy, absorbed perhaps in
religious duties or fearful of involvement, pass by; the half-caste
heretic stops, comes near and sees the wounded one, is moved with
pity and responds with immense generosity and practicality. Here is
a powerful picture of prayer in action, encountering and responding to the crucified Christ in wounded ones of our world.

Reflect and pray

Christ in the dust,
you lie there
stripped of all dignity
with dark blood seeping from jagged wounds:
are you dead?

Christ in the dust,
have I passed by
like the priest and the Levite,
busy with my life,
afraid to get involved?

Christ in the dust,
thank you for the brave ones
who reach out in utter compassion,
forgetting the risk or the cost,
tending your wounds, anointing your body,
lifting you up and bringing you to a safe place.

Christ in the dust,
confront me with my fears and indifference,
and by your Spirit, stir up within me
true love, deep compassion and determined action,
that I may love my neighbour as myself,
love them as you love me.

19 Martha and Mary

Read Luke 10:38–41.

> ... *a woman named Martha welcomed him into her home. She had a sister named Mary, who sat at the Lord's feet* ... (Luke 10:38–39)

Jesus continues his journey to Jerusalem, teaching and revealing the secrets of the kingdom on his way. Entering a village, he is welcomed into the house of Martha and Mary. The disciples who travel with him are apparently left outside, as Jesus enters into the women's house to share Martha's hospitality.

Later in Acts Peter announces that the outpouring of the Holy Spirit is on men and women alike (Acts 2:17–18), fulfilling the words of the prophet Joel. Luke emphasises the equal response of women and men to the good news; for example, in Acts he tells how the people of Samaria responded to Philip's message about the kingdom of God and the name of Jesus Christ, and 'were baptised, both men and women' (Acts 8:12). In both books he often balances stories about men with those about women.

Here the story of Martha and Mary forms a powerful affirmation of the totally equal and fully valid place of women among the followers and disciples of Jesus. Martha shows herself to be an example of faith by her welcome of Jesus, but this welcome is marred by her distracted attempt at hospitality and her resentment towards her sister. So the reader is directed to the sister, Mary, who sits at the feet of Jesus (the traditional place of a male disciple) and listens to what he has to say. At odds with the expectations of the time, which placed women in the background, in the kitchen, Mary claims her place as a disciple of Jesus. She is accepted by Jesus as a true disciple, listening to him in a way that some of his male disciples often failed to do. In the previous chapter, in the story of the transfiguration, the disciples are told by the voice from heaven to listen to Jesus (Luke 9:35). Mary listens and so Jesus tells the distracted Martha, 'Mary has chosen the better part, which will not be taken away from her' (10:42).

So often this passage is interpreted as a contrast between activists and contemplatives. The reality is that Christian activists and contemplatives alike need to welcome Jesus like Martha and sit at his feet like Mary – listening, seeking his will, knowing his love for each and for all, and acting upon this in their daily lives.

Reflect on the welcome these women gave to Jesus and your own listening to him

Lord Jesus,
we thank you for Martha, the hospitable one,
    and we thank you for Mary,
who listened and learnt your way.
We honour them and all women of love and faith
    and we seek to be open to your coming,
    your word to us and your way for our lives.

Lord Jesus,
we invite you into our homes,
    the places of our being.
We have much to do:
    show us what we must do
    and what we must set aside.
We have many things:
    show us how to share what we have and to let go
        of that which possesses us.
We are surrounded by events and voices and noise:
    help us to listen for your voice,
    your word, your silence.

Lord Jesus,
we are anxious about our lives,
worried and distracted over many things:
    help us to centre our hearts
    on the way of your kingdom,
    to carry your peace in our being
    and make peace in our world.

20 Lord, teach us to pray

Read Luke 11:1–4.

He was praying in a certain place … (Luke 11:1)

Luke's interweaving of prayer, teaching and action reaches a new climax with a story of how Jesus shares with his disciples what we know as the Lord's Prayer. The story of Martha and Mary has introduced the need to listen at the feet of Jesus, to learn from him like Mary who 'has chosen the better part' (10:42). Now the disciples put that instruction into practice as they watch Jesus pray. One of their number – unnamed and representing all – asks Jesus, 'Lord, teach us to pray as John taught his disciples.'

In Luke's gospel, the request arises from the way Jesus is praying, once again withdrawing with his followers to 'a certain place'. This contrasts with the way Matthew's gospel includes the Lord's Prayer within a section on prayer in the great Sermon on the Mount (Matthew 6:9–10). Matthew emphasises Jesus as the teacher or the new lawgiver, sitting down on the mountain to teach his disciples (Matthew 5:1). Luke instead wishes to encourage his readers not simply to follow the words of Jesus, but to follow his example: to pray not simply as he taught, but as he prayed.

Luke also recognises that the teaching of prayer follows a long tradition: Jesus is asked to teach his followers *as John the Baptist had taught his disciples* (and as other rabbis had done in the past). Jesus stands within this tradition – and Luke is respectful of the tradition – but Jesus brings a new depth and intensity to the reality of prayer.

The unknown disciple asked, 'Lord, teach *us* to pray.' Part of the training that Luke provides is to encourage each of us to think of ourselves in terms of 'us' rather than 'me' – to regard ourselves in connection with others rather than individually. Such community thinking has great power, though it can have the danger of either swamping the individual or developing into a closed exclusivism. Jesus counters both dangers by upholding the value of each person and challenging each way the community may become closed and self-serving. There must be no judging of others, no hierarchies of goodness, no looking down on others, no exclusion of humanity; more than that, our sense of connection must lead into action – the life of the kingdom day by day.

Reflect and pray

Lord, teach us to pray
with the whole of our being,
   bodies stilled and centred,
   minds focused on your way,
   hearts warmed by your grace.

Lord, teach us to pray
with the whole of your people,
   connecting to your followers
      of every time and place,
   connecting to your Church in all its varied faces,
   connecting to the world with all its joy and agony.

Lord, teach us to pray
in the power of your Spirit,
   as children of one dear God,
   as brothers and sisters in Christ
   as sinners forgiven and forgiving.

Lord, teach us to pray
   to you,
   with you,
   in you,
   this moment,
   this life,
   this eternity.

21 Friend indeed

Read Luke 11:5–13.

'... knock, and the door will be opened for you.' (Luke 11:9)

A man knocking at the door of a friend, tucked up in bed with his family, late in the evening, is a bold picture to use to describe our praying to the mystery we call 'God', but then Jesus is very willing to be bold in his pictures of prayer. It is a story drawn from the Palestinian folk traditions of his time. Like many of Jesus' pictures, there is an element of contrast intended in the story. If the unwilling friend will eventually respond simply because of the man's persistence in knocking, how much more will God, our true friend, respond to our asking, seeking and knocking.

Yet alongside the contrast are other elements to explore. What does it mean to have God as our friend? What is the bread that is required (the three loaves)? What is the door that we have to knock against? What should our response be when God seems to be asleep? In this story the disciples are first and foremost encouraged to put their utter trust in God: 'Ask and it will be given you, search and you will find, knock and the door will be opened to you' (11:9). Trust sometimes falters – we become unsure of God's friendship – so alongside this is the need for persistence. Luke's Greek word for 'persistence' in fact means 'shamelessness'. While God, the friend, may be hurrying down the stairs to open the door, we may feel that we have been standing outside for ages, so Luke encourages us to stay there and to put to one side our natural impatience. The call for persistence/shamelessness is repeated in the parable of the widow and the unjust judge (18:1–8), an even more vivid call to 'stick in there'.

Reflect and pray

My friend,
I knock and knock,
embarrassed by the echoing sound at this late hour,
anxious of what the neighbours may think,
worried that you may not come,
that the door will remain closed to my hammering.

I stand and wait,
listening for signs of your wakefulness,
sounds from within your dwelling,
the rattle of bolts, the echoes of footsteps.
I call out, I plead,
unsure of my own voice,
yet desperate that you may hear my cry.
I shout,
though the scream is silent within me.
I am hungry,
hungry for the bread you alone can give,
thirsty for that word you alone can speak.
Open the door ... open the door ... open the door.
Give me bread, not just enough for myself,
but bread that I can share with the hungry people,
your thirsty children.
Do not sleep, my friend.
Do not ignore my call.
Open the door ... open the door ... open the door.

My friend,
You come, I hear your step, your voice from within.
You come and I am overwhelmed by the life you give,
the joy you share, the hunger you satisfy.
The door has been opened.
The bread has been broken.
Thank you, God of grace, my friend indeed.

(Further passage: Luke 11:14—12:21. Reflect on the fierce light of Jesus' words and actions in the face of opposition and controversy.)

22 Let us look

Read Luke 12:22–34.

'Consider the ravens … Consider the lilies …' (Luke 12:24a, 27a)

Following his release from captivity as a hostage in Beirut, John McCarthy found the process of returning to the UK and readjusting to life at home immensely difficult. In the book *Some Other Rainbow*, he tells of how he was watching the birds from his window at RAF Lyneham:

> *It was still very strange to be 'free'. So many things were going through my mind, so many events and plans to try to put into place, that at times my brain just seized up and filled with a dense, grey cloud. I felt physically paralysed as well. At one point, I found myself stalled by the sitting-room window, staring at some birds hopping around on the grass. After a few minutes I was aware of feeling calm and relaxed again and realized that it was because I had started concentrating on the birds, fascinated by the way they pecked at the ground for food. I made a mental note that whenever I blanked out all I had to do was observe the natural world, letting its mystery change my perspective.* [47]

Looking and seeing is such a key theme in the gospel. Jesus begins his ministry by using words from Isaiah promising 'recovery of sight to the blind' (4:18). Later he tells his disciples, 'Blessed are the eyes that see what you see!' (10:23), while the tragedy for many is that they look and see nothing (8:9). True spiritual looking is not easy. Too often we ourselves get in the way; our distracted minds, our fixed agendas, our presumptions and prejudices, our self-centredness prevent us from truly looking and truly seeing.

So Jesus invites his distracted, worried, self-absorbed disciples to look at the natural world and learn its lessons. In the ordinary birds of the air and the short-lived grass of the meadows are lessons to be learnt, patterns of life and beauty that put our preoccupations into a true and proper perspective. Life is bigger than humanity, bigger than all our thoughts and worries, achievements and projects. More than that, according to Jesus, life is ultimately held in the care of a loving Creator, one who in the language of poetry feeds the birds, clothes the grass, counts each hair on our heads and each hour of our lives and knows all our needs.

But Jesus does not stop there. He challenges his disciples to look to the kingdom – God's intention for this world he created, to strive for this reality above all else. He wants them, and us, to allow God's reality and desire to be at the centre, the treasure of our lives around which all else will take its true place.

Reflect and pray

Let us be still and turn from our anxious thoughts
      and petty schemes and let us look.
Let us, by the Spirit's power, look again and look deep.
Let us look at nature with all its strange wonders.
   Look at the birds in speedy flight
      or searching patiently for seeds or worms,
      nesting in the tall trees
      or simply singing for delight
   Look at the meadow grass
      with its spectrum of greens,
      dotted with colours enough for Joseph's coat.
   Look at the wildflowers – their rich colours,
      curving shapes and delicate textures,
      far surpassing Solomon's finery
      or any designer clothes of today.
   Look at nature and see God's hand in creating
      and sustaining, moment by moment,
      the very fabric of existence.

Let us look at ourselves and the foolishness
    of our lives – our attempts to control all,
    to have all, to know all.
  Look and laugh at our folly.
  Look and change our ways.

Let us look at God, who like a loving parent
    holds and feeds, knows all our needs,
    from the basics of bread and warmth
    to the more basics of love and purpose.
  Look at God, the invisible one made visible in Jesus.
  Look and give thanks for the Creator's care,
    the Saviour's love, the Spirit's help.

Let us look for signs of God's kingdom – to seek
    that joyful reality above all else.
  Look and pray and work and strive
    for that just peace that is God's Way,
    for our world and for our lives.

*(Further passage: Luke 12:35—14:35. Reflect on Jesus' call to alertness
and action in the face of end times, his parables of the mustard seed and
guests at a banquet, and his teaching on discipleship.)*

23 Lost sheep

Read Luke 15:1–7.

> *'Rejoice with me, for I have found my sheep that was lost.'* (*Luke 15:6b*)

A simple story like Jesus' parable of the lost sheep can speak in different ways according to the context in which it is told. For Matthew the story of the lost sheep (Matthew 18:10–14) has a deep pastoral message encouraging the Church of his time to seek out those 'little ones' who have wandered from the Way and need to be drawn back into the flock. But for Luke the story has a more universal reach and missionary impetus. It arises from the Pharisee's complaint at Jesus' ministry to people on the edge – 'tax collectors and sinners'. It is about God's universal search for lost humanity, Jesus' invitations to others to join in that search and the joy that comes from people being found and carried home by God. Luke's telling of the parable has two details not in Matthew. First, on finding the lost sheep the shepherd places it on his shoulders and carries it home, perhaps an echo of God carrying his people (Hosea 11:3). Second, on returning home the shepherd invites his neighbours to share his joy. 'The glad tidings of God's love for the penitent sinner proclaimed by Jesus' is Luke's favourite theme, 'and into this parable that theme is concentrated'.[48]

Who is the lost sheep and who are the ones that are not lost? In the strange statistics of heaven, one lost sheep found brings greater joy than ninety-nine who have not strayed. Perhaps this is because for Luke the ninety-nine 'righteous persons who need no repentance' do not exist. Repentance – turning to God and taking up one's cross daily – is a necessary action for all people, Jew and Gentile alike. All are sinners, all are in need of God's gracious loving acceptance; none can rely on their own righteousness.

Reflect and pray

God, whose likeness we bear,
you never cease to search us out,
never cease to look for your lost children,
the sheep of your flock.
And when at last we are found in you,
you carry us on your shoulders,
singing and triumphant.
You draw others into the celebration
and spread your joy through heaven itself.
So, dear Lord, seek out your lost sheep of today.
Despite the pain and the cost,
enter the hard places of this earth, the places
   where hope has died,
   where faith is mocked,
   where love is abused.
Call those found in you to follow you there
to share the work of search and rescue
in the name of Jesus,
the shepherd who gave himself to the wolves
that we might live.

24 A woman and a coin

Read Luke 15:8–10.

> 'What woman having ten silver coins, if she loses one of them, does not light a lamp, sweep the house, and search carefully until she finds it?'
> (Luke 15:8)

How did Luke's traditional male readers react to the picture of God being like a peasant woman looking for a lost coin – one among ten? God like a woman lighting a lamp to search out the lost piece of metal? God getting in among the dust to sweep the corners to find this disc that seems to have had a mind of its own? Did they consider it belittling of God (the Father Almighty)? Did they consider it belittling of their own dignity and independence? Or did they miss its radical nature? Of course the richer women among Luke's hearers – those who provided their homes as meeting places – might have felt the image inadequate too. It may have seemed to be a far too domestic picture of the feminine, too trivial a story for the mystery of the glorious God.

Yet this is the kind of story that Jesus tells to get under his listeners' skin – to open up a picture of a God who laughs for joy when the lost thing is found and cannot resist calling in friends and neighbours to share in the celebration.

And what of us today? Are we above this image of God as a peasant woman wielding a lamp and a broom? Is it too crude for our sophisticated tastes? In 1991 Carol Schersten La Hurd interviewed Arab Christian women in relation to this parable, recognising that these women live in a culture that has many parallels with that of first-century Palestine. The women showed little interest in Jesus' apparent use of a female image for God. 'Instead their comments focused on the act of searching and the reasons for its intensity.'[49] They could identify with the need to restore wholeness and order – and the naturalness of celebrating with other women. One commented, 'Whenever we lose something we pray before and after finding it.'[50]

Perhaps we can allow the intensity and joy of the picture to touch us, as we pray to the one who sweeps through our lives. The seeking of God is echoed in the hymn 'Come down, O Love divine, seek thou this soul of mine'.[51] This hymn celebrating the work of the Holy Spirit is based on words of Bianco da Siena, a Christian mystic of the fifteenth century, who experienced the passionate searching of God's Spirit.

Reflect and pray

Holy Spirit, sweep through the dust of my life:
  Come down, O Love divine,
  seek thou this soul of mine.
Lighten the darkness that surrounds me
and the darkness within me;
expose my false ways and foolish pride:
  Come down, O Love divine,
  seek thou this soul of mine.
Sweep through the dust and debris,
the accumulation of knowledge
and memory and possession;
expose my childlike vulnerability:
  Come down, O Love divine,
  seek thou this soul of mine.
Find me, lift me up, restore me
to wholeness and hope,
to the purpose you have for me:
  Come down, O Love divine,
  seek thou this soul of mine.
The search is over!
Celebrate your find, your victory!
I am yours and you are mine:
  Come down, O Love divine,
  seek thou this soul of mine.
Dwell within me, Holy Spirit, my love and my joy.

25 Coming to our senses

Read Luke 15:11–24.

> 'Let us eat and celebrate; for this son of mine was dead and is alive
> again; he was lost and is found!' (Luke 15:24)

Here we come to the greatest of all parables, one that has much to
say on a purely human level about relationships, but even more
when related to the reality of the God whom Jesus demonstrated
in word and deed. The traditional title of 'the parable of the
prodigal son' does not do the story justice. It is the story of two
sons, not one; but above all it is the story of a father in his love for
his two sons. Joachim Jeremias calls it 'the parable of the Father's
love'.[52] That is the context in which we need to read the story of
the two sons – two very different characters, each in their own way
estranged from their father.

The story of the younger son speaks especially powerfully to
our Western secular society, in its 'taking leave of God' and 'doing
its own thing', its distancing of itself from the Father and its
recklessly squandering of the planet. People of faith have not been
immune from this abandonment of the Maker, this rejection of
responsibility to God. Often people of faith live much of their lives
in a very similar secular way, choosing and consuming without
reference to the Creator and the sacred heritage of this planet.

For the younger son disaster ensues, as the money runs out and
he is forced to undertake the most menial of work, degrading
himself as a Jewish boy by feeding the pigs – unclean animals in
Jewish eyes – and even eating their food.

Then at the point of total need and absolute poverty, the crucial
breakthrough happens, as he 'comes to his senses' (or literally
'comes to himself'). He remembers his father and his home.
Remembrance leads to return, though he expects – or rather

hopes – only to be treated as a servant, certainly not as a son. He returns having in his own eyes forfeited any rights before his father; no longer fit to be called a son, he hopes against hope that he will be accepted as a servant.

The surprise of the story is the father who runs out to meet his child when he sees him in the distance, embraces and kisses him and calls for celebration. The joy and love of the father is the real emphasis of the story, more fundamental than the actions of either of the sons. For Luke, this speaks of God's reckless embrace and absolute joy over his lost children being found, the dead being raised.

Reflect and pray

We have taken our Father's inheritance.
Outgrown the divine care, we go our own way.
Escaping God's home,
we attempt to make our own world.
With abandon we spend creation's riches,
bringing desert where once forests stood so proud
and melting icecaps with our heat.

People are hungry,
        hungry for food, for love, for hope;
and we watch, distant and helpless,
knowing our own emptiness.

Where shall we go?
Faith looks like slavery, a set of rules and rituals,
bitter guilt and hard duty.
Surely we are free and glad to be?

Yet our minds ache and are unsettled.
We seek all the securities, insurance for the future
and reassurance for the now.
We fill our lives with more and more,
but still stay empty.

But is there another way?
What if we come to our senses?
What if we journey back to God who is already
coming to meet us?
What if we allow ourselves to be embraced by God?
What if we share in God's feast of hope
and celebration?

The lost can be found.
The dead can rise to new life.
Thanks be to God.

26 The older son

Read Luke 15:25–32.

> *Then the father said to him: 'Son, you are always with me, and all that*
> *is mine is yours. But we had to celebrate and rejoice, because this brother*
> *of yours was dead and has come to life; he was lost and has been found.'*
> *(Luke 15:31–32)*

It is made clear at the beginning of the great 'parable of the Father's love' that this is a story of a man and his two sons, but the second son is not actually introduced into the story until what seems like its end. The younger son has returned and has been welcomed and embraced by the father. Now all that is required is that the older son shares in the celebration and the story can end.

Instead the story takes a new twist as the older son reacts not with joy and relief at his brother's return but with anger and bitterness. The son is angry at his brother – disowning him and naming him to the father as 'this son of yours' – and angry towards his father for welcoming him back. Years of pent-up resentment overflow in his angry speech, one of the most vivid pictures of family breakdown ever written in just a few lines.

Some commentators, on seeing this new theme, have even argued that originally this was a separate story; parables, they say, are only meant to make one point. Yet that is to underestimate the storytelling skills of Jesus and Luke. Here is a story with two sons and two themes, yet one father and one love. 'Even though it is a two-peaked parable, the central figure is the father.'[53] The three parables of this chapter all emphasise God's joy in response to those who recognise their need of him and return to him. However, they are also told to challenge those who do not share that joy – who look askance at Jesus' attitude to outcastes and sinners. Luke introduces the parables by telling how tax collectors and sinners were coming to listen to Jesus: 'and the Pharisees and the scribes were grumbling and saying "This fellow welcomes sinners and eats with them" ' (15:2).

Here in the second part of Jesus' story of the father and the two sons, we are given a picture of the father pleading with the older son to share his joy. It is a challenge to all people of faith who construct in their minds a god who is a judgemental tyrant rather than the Loving Parent, and who see themselves as that god's grudging servants, rather than as God's beloved children.

Reflect and pray

Father who is a stranger to me,
I stand outside and refuse to come in,
angry at your foolish love for my brother,
jealous of the joy
    that son of yours has received from you,
doubtful that you love me in that way,
resentful of the dutiful faith
    I have pursued all these years,
suspicious that the celebration will cost me dear.
I stand outside and refuse to come in.

So, Father, so full of strange grace,
you come out to meet me,
reaching out with that same foolish love,
calling me child, giving me all
and calling me to share in the celebration
of the lost being found,
the dead being raised to new life.

Father, always with me,
I who have travelled nowhere in my faith am lost.
I who have risked nothing in my love am dead.
I stand outside, but want to come in.
Restore me to yourself, renew your life within me.
Take from me my anger, jealousy, doubt,
    resentment and suspicion

and bring me home, that I may know your joy
and share in the banquet of your grace and mercy.

(Further passage: Luke 16 1–35. Reflect on Jesus' parable of the shrewd dishonest steward and his words, 'You cannot serve God and wealth.')

27 Children of Abraham

Read Luke 16:19–31.

'At his gate lay a poor man named Lazarus, covered with sores.' (Luke 16:20)

Here is a parable addressed to all the children of Abraham to remind them of their common origin and responsibility to each other. It is essentially about another closed system. Just as the foolish rich builder (12:16–21) becomes closed to the reality of God (the God of life and death), so the rich man here becomes closed to the needs of his fellow human beings, and to the witness of his nation's faith. He closes his eyes to the beggar outside his gates and he and his relatives have closed their ears to the witness of Moses and the prophets. Moses served the God who heard the cry of his people in slavery and came to set them free. The prophets are concerned above all with issues of justice, with far more verses relating to such issues than those concerning personal salvation: 'Let justice flow down like waters and righteousness like an everlasting stream' (Amos 5:24). Wealth and the self-concern that often goes with it have blocked the rich man's ears to this fundamental message.

In closing his gate on the beggar Lazarus, the rich man effectively creates an impenetrable chasm between himself and the poor. It is little wonder that the chasm continues in the story's picture of the afterlife. But now, reflecting the message of the Magnificat, their fortunes are reversed: God 'has brought down the powerful from their thrones and lifted up the lowly; filled the hungry with good things and sent the rich away empty' (1:52–53). Now the unnamed rich man is begging Lazarus to bring a drop of water to cool his tongue. It is a crude picture, but there to shock rich hearers out of their complacency.

Reflect on the great figures of the faith mentioned in this story

Father Abraham, remind us of our place within your family – your covenant of blessing for all the families of the earth. Keep the gates of our hearts open to our sisters and brothers in poverty.

Brother Moses, point us to the great 'I AM' who hears the cry of the people, knows their suffering and comes to their rescue. Open our ears to the cries of those enslaved today.

Great Prophets of the past and the present, confront us with your righteous anger at the bitter injustices of our time. Open our minds to your message of restoration and renewal.

Brother Lazarus, dying in poverty yet raised to glory, humble us in our self-seeking lives, our complacent well-being. Bring us repentance and open our lives to new hope.

Lord Jesus, the one who rose from the dead and can bring new life to all, free us from all that binds us and lead us in your way of sacrificial love and fierce compassion.

(Further passage: Luke 17:1–10. Reflect on Jesus' call to forgive and the apostles' plea to Jesus to increase their faith.)

28 Were not ten healed?

Read Luke 17:11–19.

> *Then one of them, when he saw that he was healed, turned back, praising God with a loud voice.* (Luke 17:15)

Jesus continues his way to Jerusalem and Luke places his unique story of the healing of the ten lepers in an unnamed village somewhere between Galilee and Samaria. Though his knowledge of Palestinian geography is uncertain, Luke wants to emphasise the mixture of Jewish and Samaritan races, races so long at odds with one another. As Jesus enters the village, ten lepers approach him keeping their distance, their different races and religions forgotten in their common need for healing. They recognise in Jesus one who can bring them God's mercy and pray to him as they would to God: 'Jesus, Master, have mercy on us.'

Jesus sees (rather than hears) the ten and that seeing leads to his words of command. To be seen by Jesus is to be seen by the One of Supreme Mercy. They have been seen by Jesus and now they are to show themselves to the priest. Jesus has spoken no word of cleansing, given no assurance of help but has gently alluded to the Mosaic regulation of Leviticus, where those healed of leprosy were required to go to the priest to have the cleansing ratified.

In simple obedience to Jesus' word the ten men go their way and on the way are made clean. Just as Jesus' seeing of them led to the healing, so one of the men's seeing of what has happened leads to a deeper healing – to salvation itself. There is no doubt Luke regards the moment of the one man's seeing and turning back as a moment of conversion. Vision and return lead on to worship and praise of God, a theme Luke repeats again and again. Jesus laments that such a response is only found in one of the ten, and a Samaritan, a foreigner, at that: 'Were not ten healed?' The nine have remained impervious to this transforming and saving moment.

Why did only one return? Perhaps the nine were anxious that the cure would not remain unless they continued on their way. Perhaps they simply forgot Jesus as they focused on their own healing. Perhaps they rationalised that their healing was going to happen anyway: after all, what had Jesus done for them apart from send them to the priest in what might have been a fool's errand. Perhaps they were caught up with all the things they had to do, and thanking Jesus was left to another time. One way or another they failed to truly 'see', failed to return to Jesus and to God in praise and thankfulness and so failed to experience that full salvation and well-being Jesus saw present in the healed Samaritan.

Reflect and pray

Lord Jesus,
you have seen us as we are,
needy of your grace and mercy.
You have healed us,
restoring us to life itself.
You have saved us
from ourselves and our fears
and the grip of evil.
You have rescued us
and led us to new joy and hope.

What can we give in return?
Yes, our obedience to your word to us,
yet we know that obedience is not enough.
In the face of your grace,
praise and thanksgiving alone are sufficient,
poured out at your feet, in wonder and love.

So we raise our voices
in worship and joy,
seeing all that you have done and all that you are.
Accept our love and praise this day
and then send us on our way,
made whole by your mercy.

(Further passage: Luke 17:20–37. Reflect on Jesus' announcement 'the kingdom of God is among you', and then the teaching about the end days.)

29 A widow's plea

Read Luke 18:1–8.

> 'And will not God grant justice to his chosen ones who cry to him day and night?' (Luke 18:7)

Luke draws on two of Jesus' parables about prayer that come from his own sources, to further explore our relationship to God and to others, and gives to each his own particular introduction. He explains that Jesus told the first story (about the widow and the judge) to remind his disciples of the need to 'pray always and not to lose heart'. The second story (about the Pharisee and the tax collector) is also about prayer, but in this case Luke's explanation is that Jesus aimed the story at those who trusted in themselves and their own righteousness and regarded others with contempt.

Our relationship to God cannot be separated from our relationship to other human beings; each affects the other. Thus an image of God as an angry judgemental and distant god is likely to influence our attitude to other people (and ourselves), while a view of other people that is careless or contemptuous will blur our picture of God.

As so often, Jesus uses contrast in his storytelling. He portrays a helpless widow pleading with a judge who cares neither for God nor for people and goes on to tell how eventually the persistence of the widow causes the judge to give in and answer her call for justice. Jesus points out that if this dishonest magistrate can be made to give justice to this woman, how much more will the just God listen to the persistent prayers of his people.

Yet underneath this simple message is the recognition that our prayers seem at times to go unanswered. In particular Luke recognised that the fulfilling of the kingdom Jesus proclaimed and enacted appeared to be delayed. Injustice, evil, sickness and death remain realities in Luke's world, as in our own. Will God hear the cries of his people?

According to Luke, Jesus assures us that God will be quick to answer, but at the same time persistence is needed. Keeping faith, not losing heart, praying shamelessly are essential to bring about that readiness for God to work among us, which opens up the kingdom in our own time and situation.

Reflect and pray

God of justice,
renew our faith in you
and our commitment to your kingdom:
your just rule,
where widows are heard and comforted,
the oppressed set free, the poor given hope.
Confront the injustice of our times
and give us courage to voice your outrage.

God of tenderness,
console and guard us,
that we may not lose heart
when your kingdom seems so distant,
your will so resisted.
Touch us with the tears of the outcastes,
the victims of the world's greed and carelessness.
Keep us praying
and keep us working for you.

God of urgent love,
hear our cry for this planet and its people.
Do not delay in helping us.
Do not let hope die.
Do not keep your Spirit from us.
Come to our aid and the aid of all your creation.

We pray in the name of the victim of injustice,
who will bring true justice,
our crucified and risen Lord, Jesus Christ.

30 The Pharisee's prayer

Read Luke 18:9–30.

'Two men went up to the temple to pray, one a Pharisee and the other a tax collector.' (Luke 18:10)

The bias of the gospel has again and again been towards the humble poor, those who have been brought low by life or by their own mistakes, but at their lowest point have recognised their need for God's mercy and help. In Luke's story, while Jesus is still in her womb, Mary sings to God her Saviour: 'He has brought down the powerful from their thrones and lifted up the lowly' (1:52).

Yet the powerful resist this 'put down', and equally the humble do not always hear the good news of God's 'raising up'. So Jesus continues to give parables to tease and challenge people with this divine truth.

Following on from the parable of the widow and the judge, where the seemingly powerful and unjust judge is worn down by the powerless but persistent widow, comes the story of the Pharisee and the tax collector, with its echoes of the parable of the father and his two sons.

The Pharisee seems at first the more natural person of prayer. At home in the temple, he stands at ease, and begins to thank God for all his good qualities, in contrast with the rest of humanity. The nominal word of thanks to God is soon dropped as he continues simply to list his achievements: '… I fast twice a week, I give a tenth of all my income.' He ends by literally talking to himself. For all his seriousness about 'religion' he has become detached from the reality of God, and distanced himself from God's children. Having exalted himself, he will, according to Jesus, be humbled, and Jesus is a willing instrument of that divine humbling.

The tax collector has none of the Pharisee's qualifications for being in the temple, and is overawed by the Divine Reality. The

whole of his body language is one of desperation and discomfort –
standing far off, eyes down, beating his breast, praying: 'God be
merciful to me, a sinner.' Echoing words of Psalm 51, here is a
prayer that is truly from the heart – no show, no make-believe, no
self-deception.

Jesus pronounces God's forgiveness and mercy for this man and
all who do likewise. So the footnote is addressed not only to the
Pharisees of Jesus' time, but to all who read or hear the gospel: 'All
who exalt themselves will be humbled, but all who humble
themselves will be exalted' (18:14). Luke rams home the point by
following the parable with Jesus welcoming little children and
then meeting a rich and morally upright ruler who is unable to let
go of his riches to give to the poor and to follow Jesus. Ultimately
all, rich and poor, Pharisee and tax collector, have to rely on the
impossibly generous grace of God: 'What is impossible for mortals
is possible for God.'

Reflect and pray

I met Jesus today.
Yes I, the Pharisee, met Jesus today
and he brought me to my knees.
I had stood before God and had felt so proud,
so content in my strong faith,
my goodness – in this rotten world,
my light – compared to other's darkness.
I had stood and remembered all I had achieved,
all the work I had done,
all the offerings I had given,
all the little sacrifices I had made for my god.

I met Jesus today
and he showed me that my god
had nothing to do with the Living God;
my light was darkness
when exposed to his fire;
my goodness empty and rotten to the core
in the fierce light of his goodness.

I met Jesus today
and he made me look again –
   look again at God in all that awesome love
      and that fearsome truth,
   look again at that person I had looked down upon,
   treated with contempt or simply passed by,
   look at myself and my need of love.

I met Jesus today
and he asked me to become like a little child,
a baby in the arms of God,
and it brought me to my knees –
God be merciful to me, a sinner.

(Further passage: Luke 18:31–43. Reflect on Jesus' third announcement of the cross to come and his encounter with the blind beggar.)

31 The one who seeks

Read Luke 19:1–10.

'Today salvation has come to this house, because he too is a son of Abraham.' (Luke 19:9)

Using material from Mark's gospel, Luke now has Jesus approaching Jerusalem for the climax of his ministry and saving work. But before the entry of Jesus into Jerusalem, he slips in one more story of Jesus saving an outcaste to illustrate another powerful text: 'The Son of Man came to seek out and save the lost' (19:10).

There is no doubt that an act of rescue and redemption takes place within this story, as Zacchaeus encounters Jesus and receives him into his home. Just as Jesus began his ministry with the great pronouncement of God's favour in Isaiah being fulfilled (4:16–21), here he pronounces, 'Today salvation has come to this house, because he too is a son of Abraham' (19:9).

The fundamental act of saving underlies the story, but blended with it are some other important Lucan themes. Luke does not oversimplify the act of salvation. Zacchaeus is a sinner – not simply in the eyes of the crowd, but in reality – but there are no words of repentance or of forgiveness. Instead that reinstatement is enacted through Jesus' self-invitation and Zacchaeus' joyful acceptance. The happiness with which Zacchaeus welcomes Jesus and the practical steps he takes to repair wrongs and to give generously are signs of the breaking in of salvation. In this the story echoes that of the woman who loved much: love and joy are visible signs of salvation at work.

Once again those who categorise people as righteous or sinners are challenged by Jesus' affirmation that Zacchaeus too is a child of Abraham. A little rich man, who has been involved in dubious dealings, can be counted among the humble poor who will receive good news and be counted among God's children.

Reflect and pray

I am small,
amid the teeming millions of this world
spinning in a space that grows ever larger.
I am small,
yet I seek you, THE GREAT ONE.
I climb to look beyond my crowded life,
scanning the horizon for the stirred dust
of your approach.
And here I meet you.
You speak your word,
inviting me to my own home,
inviting me to know you, where I am.

I come eagerly to greet you, THE GRACIOUS ONE,
who has come into my midst and into my heart.
I am rich, yet lost.
There is so much to repair and repay,
so much injustice of which I am part.
Yet you kindly, gloriously, accept
my fumbling attempts to make good.
You claim me as a child of Abraham,
part of your family, a brother-sister dear to you.

Thank you, THE SEEKING ONE,
who became poor that I might be truly rich
and lost your life, that I might find mine, in you.

*(Further passage: Luke 19:11–27. Reflect on Jesus' parable of slaves
entrusted with money while the master is away.)*

32 Lament over Jerusalem

Read Luke 19:28–48.

> *'If you, even you, had only recognised on this day the things that make for peace!' (Luke 19:42)*

Lament seems to be a particularly appropriate form of prayer to rediscover in our own times, as we contemplate the continued violence and injustice in our world and the threats to the planet itself. Luke includes an element of lament to surround the brutal killing of Jesus, with criminal and centurion speaking of Jesus' innocence (23:41, 47) and onlookers reacting with horror (23:48). However, the chief lament offered within the gospel is the lament of Jesus not at his own fate but at that of Jerusalem. Responding to the women who in compassion weep for him, he tells them to weep instead for themselves and their children: 'If they do this when the wood is green, what will happen when it is dry?' (23:31). The seeds of oppression and conflict are there in the killing of Jesus that will culminate in the violent suppression of the Jewish rebellion by the Roman army and the destruction of the Jerusalem temple.

The triumphal entry of Jesus into Jerusalem culminates in the disciples singing 'Blessed is the king who comes in the name of the Lord' (19:38). But this king is not a political Messiah come to drive out the Romans, rather One who is a sign that will be opposed by many, a Saviour coming in peace, a light to all nations. During Jesus' first visit to Jerusalem as a babe in arms, Mary is told of a sword that will pierce her soul (2:35). Now, in this final visitation, he weeps as he sees the city, recognising the spiral of violence that lies before it. Prophetically addressing the city as a whole, he cries, 'If you, even you, had only recognised on this day the things that made for peace.' The Pharisee's attempt to silence the disciples, which occurs between the triumph and the tears, is placed as an indication of what lies ahead: the attempt to silence Jesus will lead to a sham trial under darkness of night, a crowd manipulated into shouting 'Crucify' and a Roman public execution.

But still the focus of Jesus' lament is the city and its people. 'If only ...' are mocking words that have haunted human beings down the centuries. In our own times we lament the many 'if onlys', the many missed moments to respond to God's call to peace and justice, integrity and grace.

Reflect and pray

If only, if only, if only ...
 Is it too late for us, Lord,
to make peace in the Middle East, Jew and Arab,
  Christian and Muslim,
to make peace in Africa, black and white,
  rich and poor,
to make peace with justice for all,
to make peace with our planet?
 Is it too late for us, Lord,
to abandon our fears and our hatreds,
to abandon the arms trade with all its profit,
to abandon the corruptions, the lies, the posturing,
  the pride and the greed,
to abandon the careless exploitation of our planet?
 Is it too late for us, Lord,
to welcome you, the one who rode into Jerusalem
  in humble peace,
to weep with you, the one who wept for your city,
to watch with you, the one who gave life on a cross,
to walk with you, the one who goes before us?
 Is it too late for us, Lord,
to speak out for the voiceless,
to speak out against the forces of fear,
to speak out for a better, humbler way?
 Is it too late for us, Lord?

Lord, touch our hearts with your tears,
strengthen our hands for your work
and guide our feet into the path of peace,
that it may not be too late for us
and this world you so love.

33 *Rejected cornerstone*

Read Luke chapters 20 and 21.

> 'Then the owner of the vineyard said, "What shall I do? I will send my
> beloved son; perhaps they will respect him." ' (Luke 20:13)

Here are two long chapters of debate, controversy and dark
prophecy, set in the context of Jesus teaching in the temple (19:47;
21:37). Destruction is in the air – the plot to kill Jesus and the
future destruction of the temple and Jerusalem. Luke darkens the
picture by removing the call to love as the greatest commandment
from Mark's collection of questions and placing it earlier in the
gospel. What remains are essentially questions of authority, linked
to the baptism of John, the paying of taxes, the resurrection and
David's son. As Jesus' parable puts all too clearly, the vineyard
owner's son has come in person and his coming produces amazement and silent attention among many. But for others it is the
ultimate interference, a threat to their own authority and the result
is violence: 'they threw him out of the vineyard and killed him'
(20:15). Jesus then speaks of violence spinning out of control,
touching all with its evil power and bringing down God's temple
itself. In the face of this Jesus calls his followers to be alert and to
pray: 'In Luke's mind prayer was the opposite of losing heart. It
signalled intense persistence.'[54]

Amidst such prophecies of doom, the widow's offering comes
as a chink of light. A tiny offering to a dying and corrupt
institution may seem meaningless, yet it hints at the power of
sacrifice and self-giving. She gives all she has to live on, a tiny
foretaste of what Jesus will do on the cross, giving his life up in love
for friend and enemy, Jew and Gentile, all humanity and creation
itself. 'The stone that the builders rejected has become the corner-
stone' (20:19).

Reflect and pray

The powers that be
are at work
plotting and suppressing,
devising and insinuating.

But you, great teacher,
will not be taken in,
not impressed by self-made glory,
the boasts of holiness,
the size of our towers and temples.

You come as the rescuer,
to turn the tables on greed and injustice,
on fear and death itself.

Lighten our darkness.
Come, Lord Jesus.

34 The desire of Christ

Read Luke 22:1–38.

'I have eagerly desired to eat this Passover with you before I suffer.'
(Luke 22:15)

The darkness gathers and the hour of Jesus' exodus approaches –
the Passover festival is near. Satan who had departed from Jesus at
the end of the wilderness temptations, waiting for an opportune
time (4:13), returns. The tempter demands to sift all of the disciples
like wheat (22:31) and begins by entering Judas (22:3), drawing
him away from Jesus, the One who prays protection for all his
disciples. Caught up in the schemes of the chief priests, Judas
begins to look for an opportunity to betray his master, away from
the protecting crowd.

The hour arrives – sundown and the beginning of the Passover
feast – and the beginning of Jesus' exodus. This is no ordinary day,
but a critical moment in the history of all humanity. It is a moment
when past, present and future intersect. The Passover commemo-
ration of the deliverance of the Hebrew people from Egyptian
bondage is echoed in the preparation for a new act of deliverance
in Jesus' death – his body given, his blood poured out, the signs of
a new covenant. Alongside this, the Passover itself looks forward to
a new deliverance, a Messiah bringing a new age. The latter part of
the Hallel, the psalms sung at Passover, includes Psalm 118, with its
words, 'Blessed is the one who comes in the name of the Lord',
words used in adapted form at the entry of Jesus into Jerusalem. In
the same way, Jesus looks to God's future, when all is fulfilled in the
kingdom of God. The future promise of the Passover – of a
Messiah and a new act of deliverance – is being fulfilled in Jesus in
this hour, but a future, eschatological dimension remains. The

meal that Jesus shares, so that his friends can 'remember' him, looks forward to the kingdom banquet, when all will be brought to completion.

Yet still the disciples have much to learn about this kingdom where God is at the centre and all are truly fed. Their uncertainty over who will betray Jesus, their dispute over who is greatest and the deluded protestations of loyalty to the death all show how far they have to travel and how much they will need these signs of grace – in bread and wine – to inspire and refresh them in the years ahead. We, in our own times and situations, are no different; we need the same signs of grace – the same simple meal in remembrance of Christ – to challenge our egos and to feed our hearts.

Reflect on the Last Supper and pray

This is your deep desire, dear Lord,
to celebrate the Passover with us,
where you yourself are the sacrificial lamb,
to feed us with bread broken
and wine poured out and poured out again;
to feed us with your very self;
for us to do with what we will,
to absorb into our very being,
to carry into our daily living,
if that is what we desire.

Forgive us our slowness to receive:
  our false promises and failed courage,
  our little denials and petty quarrels,
  our concern for our own status,
  our unwillingness to give and serve
in the face of your overwhelming love.
Forgive us and restore us to yourself.
Pray for us, that our faith may not fail,
that we may turn back to you,
and strengthen our brothers and sisters.

Grant that we may eat at your table
in the company of all your frail disciples
of every time and place,
now in our own day
and in the day your kingdom is fulfilled.

35 Sleeping?

Read Luke 22:39–46.

'Why are you sleeping? Get up and pray …' (Luke 22:46)

Here at Gethsemane we reach one of the great icons of prayer in the gospel and Luke approaches the story with reverent awe. The picture he portrays is far from the idea of prayer as a satisfying spiritual exercise, there to boost our self-esteem. Here, prayer is once again real struggle, as in the story of the temptations at the very beginning of Jesus' ministry.

Luke adds a picture of an angel coming from heaven to strengthen Jesus at this vulnerable time and his sweat falling to the ground like great drops of blood. As we have noted, these two verses are not contained in all ancient manuscripts and it is quite possible that a devout scribe added them for greater effect. Still, it is also possible that Luke himself added this picture to strengthen the drama of what to him is the critical moment of anguish for Jesus. Here in Luke's eyes is the moment when Jesus faces the enormity of what lies ahead of him. The inner struggle that Mark and Matthew portray on the cross as Jesus cries 'My God, my God, why have you forsaken me' takes place in this moment of decision. Thereafter Jesus faces the cross with calm and compassionate determination, speaking words of forgiveness to his torturers, words of promise to the penitent thief and committing himself into God's hands in a final prayer.

The real struggle – the final temptation – takes place here in the garden, as Jesus enfolds his will into the mysterious, loving and awesome will of his Father:

'Father, if it be possible,
take this cup from me,
but not my will
but yours be done.'

This for Luke is the great pattern of prayer that Jesus is teaching his followers, by painful example. The disciples are unable to keep up with Jesus as he enters this darkness of prayer; instead of praying with him and for him they slip into sleep. Luke softens the criticism of the disciples by adding that they slept because of grief. But still Jesus questions them, 'Why are you sleeping?', and challenges them to learn to pray that the trial he is undergoing may not overwhelm them.

Reflect on the disciples' sleeping and Jesus' praying

Are we sleepwalking through reality, dear Lord?
Closing our eyes to your suffering
in the betrayed ones,
the starving ones,
the forgotten ones?
Turning our backs on your call to face evil head on,
to confront injustice,
to act to rescue this darkened world?

Are we sleepwalking through reality, dear Lord?
Preferring trivial games to the real task of living?
Opting for the comfortable way, the easy half-truths,
reassuring platitudes and false hopes?
Forgetting the cost of grace?

Are we sleepwalking through reality, dear Lord?
Taking all we can get from this planet
and betraying generations to come?
Prolonging our lives to the nth degree
and failing to give life to others?

Are we sleepwalking through reality, dear Lord?
Afraid to own that grief and fear we feel?
Afraid to hope for greater things,
that dying love that lives?

Wake us up, Lord of Gethsemane.
Challenge our feeble praying
with your mighty prayer,
'not my will but yours be done'.
Shame our selfishness.
We pray that we may not face the testing
you endured.
But we pray too for strength and purpose
to meet whatever life may bring,
to meet it with faith and courage
and that grace you knew and shared
in a garden long ago.

36 The hour

Read Luke 22:47—23:56.

'But this is your hour, and the power of darkness!' (Luke 22:53)

Jesus enters the time of trial that he alone can face – and from which his followers must pray to be saved. From this point on the suffering and death of Jesus is inevitable. The die has been cast; all the elements of rejection and betrayal on the one hand and loving obedience and sacrifice on the other are in place. The hour of darkness has arrived.

The disciples' attempt at violent resistance is promptly put to a stop by Jesus. 'No more of this,' says the one who came as the new dawn to give light to those under the shadow of darkness and to guide our feet into the way of peace.

Yet, paradoxically, Jesus – the dawn, the sun of righteousness – enters the utter darkness of brutality, torture, mockery, cruelty and death. Paradoxically, Jesus the innocent one (and declared innocent again and again) dies the criminal's death. Luke does not attempt to explain this in theological or doctrinal terms. He omits, for example, Mark's reference to Jesus' death as a ransom. But this does not mean that he has no theology of the cross. In fact the cross is central to Luke's gospel; it is a necessity at the heart of Jesus' way of self-giving love – the way of true, upside-down, world-shaking glory. Luke explores this not in theological terminology but in a series of encounters with Jesus as he walks the way of the cross. The way of the cross is shown to be:

- The way of non-violence – in Jesus' healing of the servant's ear.
- The way of compassion – in Jesus' turning and looking at Peter, who has just denied him three times.

- The way of protest at corrupt human powers – in Jesus' encounter with the chief priests, challenging their religious powers with his vision of God's glory, and Pilate, mediator of the great Roman power, who is shown to be utterly powerless in this situation.
- The way of forgiveness – in Jesus' words of forgiveness from the cross to those who crucified him.
- The way of rescue – in Jesus' words of promise to the criminal.
- The way of glory – as the centurion sees Jesus' death, declares him innocent and praises God.

The very powerlessness of Christ is shown to be truly powerful. Far from resisting and struggling against what is inflicted on him, he drinks the cup of suffering. He looks not to himself but to the people around and ultimately to the One who has asked him to drink this cup.

So the drama ends with Jesus quietly commending himself into his Father's hands. The one who allowed himself to be handed over 'into human hands' (9:44) now places himself into the hands of the Father. Using a verse of Psalm 31 which may have been used as an evening prayer, his words express utter trust and confidence in God: 'Father into your hands I commend my spirit' (23:46).

As the risen Lord will explain to Cleopas and his companion, 'Was it not necessary that the Messiah should suffer these things and so enter his glory?' (24:26).

Reflect and pray

Lord Jesus,
the hour is not yours.
It is the hour of the powerful,
the violent, the corrupt;
an hour when you are seized
and taken, led away, denied,
mocked and beaten,
blindfolded and insulted.

You are sent back and forth,
sport of mockers.
Your fate lies in the whim of the crowd
and the calculation of a weak politician.
You are condemned,
led away to be put to death,
stripped of your clothing,
nailed to a cross.
This hour is not yours.
It is the hour of darkness,
where even the sun's light fails.
Yet ...
Yet through the failure of Peter,
we see your look of compassion.
Over the mocking voices,
we hear your words of forgiveness.
In your searing pain,
we glimpse your promise of paradise.
In the darkest hour,
we know your innocence.
In your silence,
we hear God's whisper of love.
In your utter powerlessness
we see the power of God.
This is your hour of triumph!
This is your hour of victory!
Thanks be to God!

37 Remember

Read Luke 24:1–12.

Then they remembered his words ... (Luke 24:8)

For Luke the handing over of Jesus, the crucifixion of Jesus, his rising again on the third day and ascending to glory are inextricably linked. They are the exodus that Jesus must accomplish so that repentance, forgiveness and the pouring out of the Spirit can take place among his followers and to the ends of the earth. The women are witnesses of this entire event: they watch the death of Jesus (23:49), they see the tomb and how his body is laid within it (23:55), and on the first day of the week they come to the tomb. Very early that morning – literally at 'deep dawn' – they come bringing the spices and ointments they prepared before the Sabbath day of rest, to anoint the body of Jesus, as 'the woman who loved much' had done long before. They see the stone rolled back, they go into the tomb and find the body has gone. As they puzzle over this they are met by two messengers in dazzling clothes. Confusion turns to terror, but the messengers bring not death but news of life: 'Why do you look for the living among the dead? He is not here, but has risen.'

The messengers ask the women to remember the words of Jesus and how he spoke of his 'exodus'. The implication is that the women have been fully included alongside the male apostles and disciples in Jesus' sharing of the gospel teaching and promises. Nothing of the essence of the Gospel has been restricted to some inner circle or male elite. The women are now most definitely part of the group and will astound the slower male apostles with their news.

For the women remember the words of Jesus, a key phrase in Luke's gospel. A fundamental element of prayer is remembering –

remembering the past acts, presence and promises of God and knowing a God who remembers us. Approaching his passion Jesus tells his followers to share bread in remembrance of him. On the cross he responds graciously to the criminal's plea: 'Jesus, remember me when you come into your kingdom' (23:42).

The apostles somehow fail to remember, despite the women telling them repeatedly the news they have received; Luke's Greek emphasises that the women didn't simply speak once to be then dismissed, but kept on saying what they had heard and remembered. Yet the harsh reality of Jesus' agonising death, and their own total failure to stand with him, somehow cloud the apostles' memories. Only the risen Lord himself is able to break open their shattered hearts and minds to his promises and enable them to know alongside the women that 'the Lord has risen indeed'.

Reflect and pray

God of faithful love,
we remember with thanks Mary Magdalene, Joanna,
    Mary mother of James and the other women
    with them, as the great witnesses of Christ's
    death and resurrection.

We remember with thanks the women
    as they watched their Saviour die,
    standing at a distance in the horror of it all.
We remember with thanks the women
    as they saw the newly cut tomb
    and the way the limp body of Jesus
    was laid out within it.
We remember with thanks the women
    as they gathered spices and ointments,
    grinding and mixing in preparation
    for their loving duty.
We remember with thanks the women
    as they rested on the Sabbath,
    obedient to the law, exhausted
    with grief and despair.

We remember with thanks the women
    as they rose early that first day,
coming with heavy hearts
    to the tomb of the beloved.
We remember with thanks the women
    as they discovered the tomb empty
and stepped within its cold walls,
    seeing that the body was gone.
We remember with thanks the women
    as they bowed their faces
before the awesome messengers of life,
    dazzling and terrifying.
We remember with thanks the women
    as they heard the message
    'Christ has risen' and recall his promises.
We remember with thanks the women
    as they tell their story
    and astound their friends.
We remember with thanks the women
    as they hold to their testimony
    despite the mockery and unbelief
    of the eleven and the rest.

God of new life,
guard us from
    forgetting your Easter good news,
    closing our minds to your resurrection truth,
    hardening our hearts to our risen Lord.
By your refreshing Spirit,
    help us to share the women's wondrous joy
    and deep hope,
that we too may tell the news of the living one.

38 Emmaus Road

Read Luke 24:13–35.

While they were talking and discussing, Jesus himself came near and went with them. (Luke 24:15)

Having begun his proclamation of the risen Saviour with the story of the women at the tomb, Luke turns next in an equally unexpected direction, focusing on two unknown disciples and their encounter with the risen Lord. The seemingly more significant appearance of Jesus to Simon Peter is only reported later, as a single verse (24:34). Instead Luke focuses on the story of Cleopas and his unnamed companion. Of their past or future role among the disciples and within the Church, Luke has no record, but he sees their story as taking us to the heart of the resurrection reality and what it can mean to every Christian disciple.

Within the story are some familiar Lucan themes: the journey, the encounter with Jesus, the honest sharing of need, the explaining of the Scriptures, the breaking of bread, the opening of eyes, the burning hearts and the hurried journey to share the good news. All these great themes are located in the dust of the road from Jerusalem to Emmaus and in the ordinary bread shared at the table of two friends.

Like all the gospel-writers, Luke gives no account of Jesus' resurrection itself. The first hints are in a stone rolled away, an absent body and an angelic message: 'Why are you looking for the living among the dead?' (24:5). The actual event of raising is surrounded in mystery, but its reality is made known in encounter, or rather a series of encounters. In Luke's gospel this builds up step by step to Jesus' final blessing of his friends on the hillside of Bethany and their worship of him. Luke's story of the two companions on the road to Emmaus fits perfectly into this glorious crescendo.

Luke carries us with him on a journey from Jerusalem to Emmaus, back to Jerusalem again, then to Bethany and then back to Jerusalem. In that journey we are carried from cold despair to burning hope, from confusion to understanding, from fear to joy, from doubt to worship. In the opening of Scripture, the breaking of bread and the sharing of news, the risen Lord makes himself known, shares his peace and prepares his friends for the task ahead.

Reflect and pray

Why, Jesus?
Why are our hopes shattered?
Why such sadness, such suffering?
Why do you walk with us as a stranger?
Why are our eyes closed to your presence?

Yes, Jesus,
our hearts are foolish and slow to believe.
Our ears are deaf to the witness of your people.
Our Bibles remain closed, despite all we read;
we fail to meet you through its pages.

Yes, Jesus,
open the Scriptures to us.
Make our hearts burn within us,
as the words become alive and real
and as you draw us to yourself.

Stay, Jesus,
it is almost evening and the day is nearly done.
Share at our table, take the bread and bless it.
Break it and meet our need
and make yourself known in the breaking.

Go, Jesus,
go before us on our journey
and help us to tell others
of the fire that burns within us
and how you fed us with the living bread.

(Further passage: Luke 24:36–43. Reflect on the third appearance of the risen Christ as he greets his startled disciples, 'Peace be with you.')

39 History's hinge

Read Luke 24:44–52 (and Acts 1:1–14).

They worshipped him, and returned to Jerusalem with great joy; and they were continually in the temple blessing God. (Luke 24:52)

Luke began his gospel in the temple in Jerusalem, with the faithful priest Zechariah offering prayers for his people. He ends the gospel where he began, with the disciples returning to Jerusalem and being 'constantly in the temple blessing God'. The place is the same, a symbol of continuity, but the atmosphere has changed utterly. The faithful but hopeless prayers of Zechariah, unexpectedly answered by God's grace, make way for the joy and exuberant worship of the followers of Jesus, the Messiah, who suffered and rose again and promises to send the Spirit to empower them and send them out as his witnesses.

Luke closes his gospel with the withdrawal of Jesus, in contrast to the reassuring final words of Jesus in Matthew's gospel, 'I am with you always, to the end of the age' (Matthew 28:19). Luke emphasises this departure because he wants to prepare his readers for his next volume, where Jesus sends the promised Spirit on his followers so that they can continue his work.

So, for Luke, the 'ascension' of Jesus into glory becomes the hinge linking the story of Jesus' ministry (in Judaea, culminating in Jerusalem) and the story of his Church's mission in his name and by his Spirit (to all nations, beginning in Jerusalem). To emphasise this, he repeats the story of the ascension at the beginning of the Acts of the Apostles. He is clear that the ending is also the beginning.

Between the two events of the ascension of Jesus and the coming of the Spirit, there is a gap – a waiting time. The risen Jesus tells his friends that they will be his witnesses, but first they must wait: 'Stay here in the city until you have been clothed with power

from on high.' The space between Jesus' going and the Spirit's
coming is not to be one of anxious activity, but rather one of joyful
praise and faithful prayer.

Reflect on the disciples worshipping in the temple

We return to the familiar place,
the holy temple
with all its history,
all its hopes and disasters,
all its glory – true and false,
the stones impregnated with prayer
yet tainted with injustice and exclusion.
Will God indeed dwell on earth?
  We come to praise our Lord, the righteous One,
  to thank our God who has acted,
    without question, beyond all human grasp.
We return to the familiar place,
remembering all our Lord did and said
within its precincts day after day,
his anger at the traders, the robbers of the poor,
his powerful words and fearsome challenges,
his courage in the face of death threats and plots.
*The stone which the builders rejected has become the
      cornerstone.*
  We come to praise our Lord, the Living Stone,
  to thank our God who acts,
    bringing life from death, victory from defeat.

We return to the familiar place,
yet we are different.
We know God is true and real,
not bound to past history, but living and life-giving,
filling us with joy and hope.
*The curtain of the temple has been ripped apart by the
      light of the cross.*
  We come to praise our Lord, the righteous One,
  to thank our God who will act,
    sending that Spirit which we seek
    and for which we wait in worship.

40 Breakthrough

Read Acts 2:1–18.

All of them were filled with the Holy Spirit … (Acts 2:4)

Luke believes in breakthrough moments – moments when the kingdom of God becomes present in a very powerful way on earth. Always self-effacing, he does not tell us of his own breakthrough moment with God. He does share those of other disciples, and they take many forms. There is the angel's message to Zechariah in the temple, to Mary in her home, to the shepherds on the hillside, to the women at an empty tomb; there is Jesus' encounter with Simon in his boat, an unnamed woman in Simon's house, Legion on the hillside, Martha and Mary in their home, Zacchaeus up the sycamore tree, a criminal on a cross, two friends journeying to Emmaus.

Pentecost is one such breakthrough moment, promised at the end of the gospel: 'I am sending upon you what my Father has promised' (24:49). It is not the arrival of the Holy Spirit, for the Spirit has been at work since creation itself, but it is such an outpouring that hearts and tongues are loosened, lives stirred and renewed and the Church born in praise and proclamation. The exclusive, narrow, particular elements of religion are swept away in the dramatic fulfilment of the very particular Hebrew prophecy of Joel:

> *In the last days it will be, God declares,*
> *that I will pour out my Spirit upon all flesh,*
> *and your sons and daughters shall prophesy,*
> *and your young men shall see visions,*
> *and your old men shall dream dreams. (Acts 2:17; Joel 2:28)*

The Holy Spirit comes not in a shower or dribble, but is poured out onto the disciples. Luke describes its coming in a series of superlatives: the Spirit comes with a sound like 'the rush of a violent wind', filling 'the entire house', with tongues of fire resting on each of the disciples gathered there; 'all of them were filled with the Holy Spirit'. The immediate result is that a crowd of onlookers gather, amazed and astonished at how the Galilean disciples are somehow overcoming all language difficulties to communicate the greatness of God. Then Peter stands up to tell them the story of Jesus and to call them to turn around and return to the God who has rushed out to meet them.

Reflect and pray

Come, Holy Spirit,
break into our lives,
gently or fiercely,
with reassurance or challenge, grace or truth.

Come, Holy Spirit,
burn in our hearts,
awakening love, releasing faith, warming love.

Come, Holy Spirit,
blow through our senses,
unsettling our cosy comfortable ways,
sending us out to share wonder and to give praise.

Come, Holy Spirit,
reawaken your people,
demolishing the walls of division
and uniting all in vision and action.

Come, Holy Spirit,
speak in our world
a language that unites, instead of dividing,
a word of peace, instead of war,
a sound of joy, instead of fear.

Come, Holy Spirit,
in power and love,
joy and wonder,
challenge and grace.

Come and stay,
the embrace of God
on our lives today. Amen.

Notes

1   Michael Quenot, *The Icon:Window on the Kingdom* (London: Mowbray, 1991), p. 15.

2   Thomas Merton, quoted in Jim Forest, *Praying with Icons* (Maryknoll NY: Orbis Books, 1997), p. 12.

3   Henri J. M. Nouwen, *Behold the Beauty of the Lord: Praying with Icons* (Indiana: Ave Maria Press, 1988), p. 14.

4   Oscar Cullmann, *Prayer in the New Testament* (London: SCM Press, 19), p. 16.

5   Joseph Fitzmyer, *The Gospel According to Luke I – IX*, The Anchor Bible (New York: Doubleday & Co., 1981), p. 244.

6   W. H. Auden, 'Prayer, Nature of' in *A Certain World: A Commonplace Book* (New York: Viking Press, 1970).

7   Jon Sobrino, 'Christian Prayer and New Testament Theology: A Basis for Social Justice and Spirituality' in Matthew Fox (ed.), *Western Spirituality: Historical Roots, Ecumenical Routes* (Santa Fe: Bear & Co., 1981), p. 80.

8   Terry Hinks, *God's Passion: Praying with Mark* (London: Darton, Longman & Todd, 2011), p. 27.

9   Meister Eckhart, source unknown.

10 James L. Resseguie, *Spiritual Landscape: Images of the Spiritual Life in the Gospel of Luke* (Peabody MA, Hendrickson Publishers, 2004), p. 5.

11 Resseguie, *Spiritual Landscape*, p. 5.

12 Fitzmyer, *The Gospel According to Luke I – IX*, p. 227.

13 Stephen Barton, *The Spirituality of the Gospels* (London: SPCK, 1992), p. 93.

14 John Whittier, 'Dear Lord and Father of mankind'.

15 Barton, *The Spirituality of the Gospels*, p. 95.

16 Barton, *The Spirituality of the Gospels*, p. 95.

17 Eduard Schweizer, *Luke:A Challenge to Present Theology* (London: SPCK, 1982), p. 93.

18 Luci Shaw, *Accompanied by Angels* (Grand Rapids MI: Eerdmans, 2006).

19 Clement of Alexandria.

20 Forest, *Praying with Icons*, p. 15.

21 Fitzmyer, *The Gospel According to Luke X – XXIV*, The Anchor Bible (New York: Doubleday & Co., 1983), p. 1443.

22   Paul Borgmann, *The Way According to Luke: Hearing the Story of Luke-Acts* (Grand Rapids MI: Eerdmans, 2006), p. 31.

23   Fitzmyer, *The Gospel According to Luke X – XXIV*, p. 1082.

24   Borgmann, *The Way According to Luke*, p. 233.

25   Simon Tugwell, *Prayer: Keeping Company with God*, Part Two (Dublin: Veritas Publications, 1974), p. 3.

26   Walter Brueggemann, *The Psalms and the Life of Faith*, ed. Patrick D. Miller (Minneapolis MN: Augsburg Fortress Press, 1995), p. 14.

27   Borgmann *The Way According to Luke*, p. 385.

28   H. J. Cadbury, *The Making of Luke-Acts* (London: SPCK, 1961), p. 267.

29   Charles Wesley, 'Love Divine'.

30   Barton, *The Spirituality of the Gospels*, p. 63.

31   William G. Morrice, *Joy in the New Testament* (Exeter: Paternoster Press, 1984), p. 91.

32   Morrice, *Joy in the New Testament*, p. 91.

33   Leon Bloy, source unknown.

34   C. S. Lewis, *Surprised by Joy: The Shape of My Early Life* (London: Geoffrey Bles, 1955), p. 224.

35   Sobrino, 'Christian Prayer and New Testament Theology', p. 110.

36   Sobrino, 'Christian Prayer and New Testament Theology', p. 88.

37   Michael Campbell-Johnston in *How I Pray*, ed. John Wilkins (London: Darton, Longman & Todd, 1993), p. 39.

38   Martin Buber, *I and Thou*, 2nd edn (Edinburgh: T & T Clark, 1958), p. 6.

39   The Westminster Confession.

40   John Betjeman, 'Christmas' from *Collected Poems* (London: John Murray, 1962), p. 189.

41   Karl Barth, *Prayer*, 50th anniversary edition (Louisville KY: Westminster John Know Press, 2002), p. 13.

42   George Caird, *Saint Luke* (Harmondsworth: Penguin, 1963), p. 43.

43   Fitzmyer, *The Gospel According to Luke I – IX*, p. 394.

44   Walter Brueggemann, *Struggling with Scripture* (Louisville KY: Westminster John Knox Press, 2002), p. 25.

45   Amy-Jill Levine, *A Feminist Companion to Luke* (Sheffield: Sheffield Academic Press, 2002), p. 12.

46   K. A. von Hase, *Geschichte Jesu* (Leipzig: Breitkopf und Hartel, 1891), p. 422, quoted in Fitzmyer, *The Gospel According to Luke X – XXIV*, p. 866.

47   John McCarthy and Jill Morrell, *Some Other Rainbow* (London: Bantam Press, 1993), p. 418.

48   J. M. Creed, *The Gospel According to St Luke* (London: Macmillan, 1930), p. 196.

49   Levine, *A Feminist Companion to Luke*, p. 250.

50   Levine, *A Feminist Companion to Luke*, p. 251.

51   Bianco da Sienna (trans. R. F. Littledale), 'Come down, O Love divine'.

52   Joachim Jeremias, *The Parables of Jesus* (London: SCM Press, 1963), p. 128.

53   Fitzmyer, *The Gospel According to Luke X – XXIV*, p. 1085.

54   Charles H. Talbert, Reading Luke: A Literary and Theological Commentary on the Third Gospel (New York: Crossroad, 1986), p. 204.

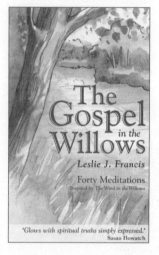

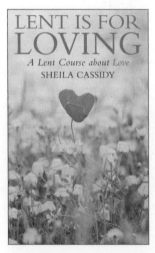

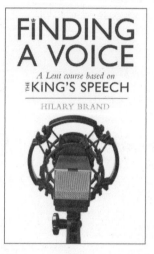